Testimonials

With passion and grace, Walt Shelton engages, challenges, and guides us in how we can each make the most of this incredible life we have been given. Sharing profound insights from personal experiences, wisdom from a variety of voices, and tools and resources for us to use, Walt encourages us to address our distractions and fears as well as articulate our life priorities throughout the seasons of our lives so that we may live meaningful and meaning-filled lives.

Rev. Dr. Susan Lowe, CT
Louisville, Kentucky
Minister of Congregational Care
Beargrass Christian Church (Disciples of Christ)

†

After getting to know Walt personally in several classes throughout law school, it was no surprise to me that his wit and wisdom would be communicated through his books. *Authentic Living in All Seasons* truly applies Walt's insight to everyday human problems like fear, time management, and stress. He offers readers his methods of self-reflection and meditation along with the gospel to help show us how we can maintain a healthy balance in life.

Devante Marshall
Houston, Texas
Former law student and now friend

In *Authentic Living in All Seasons*, Walt's own lifestyle is evident as he considers what it means to live, in a practical sense, and he encourages his readers to do the same. Walt's emphasis on justice as a crucial part of our expression of our faith, and his model of principled, qualitative, and mindful living is essential for all Christians. Additionally, his practical and systematic approach makes authentic living feel not only attainable, but also imperative for the life of both individual Christians and the church at large.

Masyn Evans-Clements
Austin, Texas
Minister for Youth and Outreach
The Church at Highland Park

✝

It is rare to find a book that genuinely feels as though it is meant for everyone. *Authentic Living in All Seasons* is among those rarities. Like Walt himself, the book embraces readers from all walks of life. Though the book is centered around the Christian faith, it certainly does not exclude a non-Christian audience. Instead, the book encourages a sense of community and oneness among its readers. It advocates for positivity with purpose and provides a refreshing perspective on daily living. Additionally, the style and tone of the writing bring a sense of warmth to the reader that is unique to Walt Shelton's work. Walt's passion for life and love of humanity is clear from the first few pages. Walt Shelton himself is an inspiration, and his work is no exception.

McKenzie Speich
Alamo Attorney
General Land Office (Austin, Texas)
Former law student and now friend

Walt is the person I think of when naming a "model" human being. He truly does walk the walk and it inevitably influences all of those around him. *Authentic Living in All Seasons* is no different. Walt takes you through the "why" of authentic and principled living, and then provides short perspectives on how we can apply it to our daily lives. Every time I open one of Walt Shelton's works, I know I am going to be motivated to view life in a more positive and directed manner. Walt also doesn't leave anyone out. While Walt is open about his Christian faith, his books are not limited to a Christian audience. With Walt's inclusivity, he encourages all of us to be more open-minded, community-based, and to realize that "God's plan" is really just one and the same for us all.

Zoë Fedde
Associate Attorney, Merritt Law
Houston, Texas
Baylor Law School Class of 2021
Former law student, research assistant, (and now) friend

†

God absolutely uses Walt Shelton as a vessel for His teachings. Walt's first book, *The Daily Practice of Life*, is a moving account of Walt's life experiences and perspectives on incorporating faith-based principles into a daily routine. My husband and I both read *The Daily Practice of Life* like a devotional and had many thought-provoking discussions regarding its contents. Walt's latest book, *Authentic Living in All Seasons*, is so deeply personal and relatable that it makes you feel seen and understood. But perhaps most importantly, his book is soul inspiring in such a way that it evokes a call to action to be the best versions of ourselves. The book takes on a wide range of complicated topics—from inclusiveness and social justice to suffering, to name a few—and provides a subtle yet dynamic, biblical perspective for evaluating these topics. The book provides a much-needed solution-oriented focus, a refreshing approach in a world that seems to often dwell on the negative. Walt points to an abundance of Scripture to illustrate just how beautiful the day-to-day bustle of life is and shows that even the "little things" we do for others can have an impact. *Authentic Living in All Seasons* is the perfect book for those that want a deep and reflective study of faith and meaningful living.

Kristen Fancher
Attorney/Owner of Fancher Legal, PLLC
Prosper, Texas
Colleague and friend of Walt Shelton
Co-Chair of the Law School Programs Committee of the State Bar of Texas, Environmental and Natural Resources Law Section with Walt Shelton

✝

Walt Shelton writes religion columns that have always felt like columns about the human experience. Sure, he'll quote Scripture and add his Christian lens to them, but at the core of his columns are this universality.

His columns often include some sage wisdom passed down from his grandfather, a person he recently met, or a dog. They are always completely relatable.

He addresses the trials and tribulations of this modern age with perspectives that feel timeless, yet he's not afraid to address the "now" around us. He's written about social justice and equity, and how we can better understand what it means to be an ally and enter spaces that might make us uncomfortable but are truly important

During this pandemic, Walt has been that calming voice guiding his reader through. He's brought elements of hope, mindfulness, and kindness to dark times. He's given us lessons in what's really important in how we want to live our lives.

The *Austin American-Statesman* readers have been blessed to get a first look at his uplifting messages for more than a decade. And now, he shares this second volume of his columns in Part II of his book with you, along with a Part I loaded with insights on the importance of keeping focused on now, dealing with fear, and using self-reflection to identify priorities and working to keep them in balance.

Sit down, grab a cup of coffee or tea, and enjoy the pearls of wisdom on every page. You'll be glad you did.

Nicole Villalpando
Specialty Editor at the *Austin American-Statesman*
Austin, Texas

✝

It is not difficult to recognize when a person lives out their calling. Whether or not Walt ever dreamed of becoming a teacher, it is evident to anyone who meets him that he was called to this profession. In the short time I have been blessed to know him, Walt has taught me how to be a good student, a good person, and a good Christian. Walt uses his gift of teaching in *Authentic Living in All Seasons* to provide readers with a guide to living a meaningful life through vulnerable personal stories, authentic self-reflection, and thoughtful discussion of the teachings of Jesus. I have no doubt that this book will have a profound effect on anyone who reads it.

Riley Rogers
Counsel at Summit Midstream Partners, LP
Houston, Texas
Baylor Law School Class of 2021
Former law student, now friend, and forever mentee of Walt Shelton

Authentic Living in all Seasons: Focused, Fearless, and Balanced by Walt Shelton could perhaps be more appropriately entitled *Authentic* Loving *in All Seasons: Focused, Fearless and Balanced.* As an author with more than thirty years of experience as a law professor and life-long student of theology, Walt challenges his reader, teaches his reader, and then provides practical and personal counsel on how to apply what he teaches. It is as if he sees his reader as a focused law student eager to learn so that the teaching can become a useful tool for their profession of life.

Walt's focus is "love" as defined and modeled by Christ. What constitutes the love of Christ? What likely misses the mark? Further, if the reader audits his or her life, is he or she loving as Christ teaches us to love?

Again, based on his life-long dedication to learning and teaching, Walt begins his book by giving his readers three useful tools for living: Focused Attention on Now; Avoiding Stagnation from Fear; and the Practice of Periodic Self-Reflection. As you read the first four chapters of his book, you will find yourself engaging in self-analysis time and again.

If you are challenged and/or concerned about the caustic "tribal" nature of our present society (e.g., party politics, homelessness, hunger, racial issues, immigration debates, denominational disputes, religious apathy), and wish to consider those issues while attempting to apply love as defined and modeled by Christ, this is a must read for you. Even though you may not always agree with Walt (a tool often used by law professors), you will walk away from this book challenged, convicted and perhaps with a changed heart of how you personally should interact with others by voice and by deed.

Johnny Merritt
Merritt Law—Owner and Attorney
Austin, Texas
Host of Popular "Shifting the Law with Johnny Merritt" Podcast

I met Walt Shelton when he taught me at Baylor Law School. Since the moment I met him, he has been a wellspring of wisdom, knowledge, and virtue. I am proud to have said that I took as many classes with him as I could. I am prouder now of the privilege to call him a friend.

I am as much a student of his now as I was in law school because of these profound books he has created. His first book, *The Daily Practice of Life: Practical Reflections Toward Meaningful Living*, struck a real chord for me, and I only read it in law school. However, in the "real world," the legal profession can be fraught with spiritual onslaught to the point where many lawyers feel completely spiritually bankrupt. There is a dearth of guided spiritual nourishment for the legal community, and it truly shows. *Authentic Living in All Seasons* brings us some necessary reflection and guidance for a profession that is expected to have all the answers to peoples' problems. And it points the finger at something that every lawyer and other person has control over: themselves. The need for introspection and personal inventory that Walt's Part I calls for from the get-go is echoed in his first book in some respects, but it now calls for a more nuanced journey toward spiritual self-care.

Wyatt E. Fraga
Associate Attorney—Anderson, Smith, Null & Stofer, LLP
Victoria, TX
Baylor Law School—Class of 2021
Former law student and now friend

In my experience, Walt Shelton embodies the highest of character traits. I appreciate his insights on living a life of authenticity and meaning because Walt knows how easy it is to lose yourself in the hustle and bustle of the modern world. Despite this, he has continuously reexamined what is meaningful in life. In *Authentic Living in All Seasons*, Walt has refined his part-parable, part-autobiographical style of writing to extend a hand to the reader and say, I know the path of life is hard, but maybe my story can help you in yours. No matter who you are, where you are from, or what you believe, Walt's words break through all the divides to envision a life of love, kindness, compassion, and care for everyone.

Brock Lewis
Houston, Texas
Associate Attorney
Baylor Law School Class of 2021
Former law student, research assistant, and now friend

✝

I have known Walt Shelton since my high school years as a friend. Now I get to know him as an author! Walt's first book, *The Daily Practice of Life: Practical Reflections Toward Meaningful Living*, is an insightful and meaningful guide to important and relevant topics that are part of daily living. In this his second book, *Authentic Living in All Seasons: Focused, Fearless, and Balanced*, Walt continues to lead readers to think deeply about the choices we make as we walk the paths of our lives. Walt introduces new and important topics. He encourages and challenges me and all of us to think about our respective personal journeys in clear, concise, and meaningful prose. Mindfulness, fear, personal change, and balance are just a few of the subjects that he guides the reader to embrace with a combination of seriousness, humor, clarity, and sincerity.

Mary Lu Breshears
Tucson, AZ
Participant in Walt's Spring 2021 six-week virtual program: "Cultural Transformation: An Open Discussion of Respect, Inclusiveness, Racial Harmony, and the Pursuit of Justice"
Long-time friend of Walt

✝

I feel Walt Shelton has a compelling desire to help his readers hear the call to discipleship. Encouragers are on short supply—not so with Walt and those of whom he speaks and writes. Every time I listen to his Sunday school lessons and read his books I cannot but feel more joyful and ready to pursue a deeper relationship with God and my fellow man. For this I am so grateful.

Donna Reisenbigler
Member of The Church at Highland Park (Austin, TX)
Member of Walt's Sunday discussion group and participant in Walt's spring 2021 six-week virtual program: "Cultural Transformation: An Open Discussion of Respect, Inclusiveness, Racial Harmony, and the Pursuit of Justice"

✝

Walt Shelton has been a mentor and friend to us for more than two decades. His support and words of encouragement allow us to overcome—and cherish—what at first might appear to be overwhelming. In his first book, *The Daily Practice of Life*, Walt expands on articles he wrote for the *Austin American-Statesman* that we can use as devotionals for meaningful living. Part II of *Authentic Living in All Seasons* is also based on expanded articles. But the first part of the book is Walt as we know him during his Sunday school class, church meetings, workshops, study groups, and retreats: Teaching and showing us how we can be mindful in the present to care for and love all, especially the poor and oppressed. Or, as the inspiration to The Church at Highland Park's vision statement boldly states, "To Follow Jesus by Embracing All."

Don and Becky Dillard
Members of The Church at Highland Park and members of Walt's Sunday discussion group in Austin, TX
Participants in Walt's Spring 2021 six-week virtual program: "Cultural Transformation: An Open Discussion of Respect, Inclusiveness, Racial Harmony, and the Pursuit of Justice"

Authentic Living in All Seasons

FOCUSED, FEARLESS, AND BALANCED

Walt Shelton

CrossLink Publishing
RAPID CITY, SD

Shelton/CrossLink Publishing
1601 Mt Rushmore Rd. Ste 3288
Rapid City, SD 57701
www.CrossLinkPublishing.com

Ordering Information:
Quantity sales. Special discounts are available on quantity purchases by corporations, associations, and others. For details, contact the "Special Sales Department" at the address above.

Authentic Living in All Seasons/Walt Shelton. —1st ed.
ISBN 978-1-63357-416-8
Library of Congress Control Number: TBD

To Roxanne, the absolute love of my life, who loves, supports, and cares for me in every way possible.

*"Teach us to pay full and focused attention
each day of Your gift of life so that we may gain
authentic wisdom as You walk with us through our
experiences." "Exercise great care in how you live
each day, as wise people, making the most of your
limited time."*

Author's paraphrase and expansion of
Ps 90:12 and Eph. 5:15-16

Contents

Foreword

When I retired in 2011 after forty years of teaching the history of religion in America at the University of Texas at Austin, I asked Walt (then I called him by his first name, Robert) Shelton to speak on behalf of my former students at a retirement celebration. His first words on that happy occasion were memorable. He looked at the audience, scowled ever so slightly, and then thundered, "I was raised in the warm embrace of the Southern Baptist Church . . . and got over it."

Those, he explained, were the words he most distinctly remembered from the classes he took with me in the mid-1970s, near the beginning of my UT career. As a cocky beginning professor, I did say that to my first students, who were mostly Texans and often either practicing or "recovering" Southern Baptists. But Walt knew that by 2011, Dr. Miller had learned a crucial life lesson: many of us never "get over" the belief traditions of our birth.

Both Walt and I were raised, a generation apart, in "the warm embrace" of that Southern Baptist Church. He grew up in Tyler, Texas, while I was raised three hundred miles to the west, in and around Graham. Both of us learned from our shared evangelical tradition that every human encounter is precious because it is an opportunity to share the "gospel," the "good news," and thereby influence another being's life. Over the past four decades, both of us, in very different ways, have become evangelists for a "gospel" that combines the best of Christianity with what I call, "the gospel of an excellent education" and the wisdom gained from life experience.

Our journeys came together in the mid-1970s at the University of Texas in Austin (UT). We worked together as Robert constructed a religion major at a university that did not offer a religion degree. I immediately recognized the tall, skinny, slightly awkward kid from Tyler as a kindred spirit. Robert was a frequent visitor to my office and, when I laid the foundations for what became the current Department of Religious Studies at UT, he served as the student representative on the committee that finally produced that department. Without Robert, I might not have become aware as early as I did of the depth and diversity of my colleagues who were primarily interested in religion and religious experience in their individual disciplines. He is, to that extent, responsible for the existence of the Religious Studies Department at UT.

While he was my student, I often thought of Robert as something like a scholarly beachcomber, carefully picking through the UT course offerings as he patched together a religion major from found bits and pieces, rather like creating a vocational mosaic. I suspect that the experience of feeling his way through those numerous options in the social sciences, liberal arts, and biblical studies helped the young Robert Shelton to discover and appreciate what Nicholai Berdyaev called, "the variety of the human condition," which was for the Russian writer the beginning and finally the essence of a true education. My sense of Robert Shelton as an undergraduate student was of an authentic Christian striving to understand the way in which he would respond to the evangelical imperative to spread "the good news." This book is the latest step in that life-long search.

After he graduated from the UT in the late 1970s, I lost contact with Robert Shelton until *Walt* Shelton showed up in 2009 at a lecture I gave on the UT campus. Since that reunion, I have worked to keep in contact with my former student, who is now a lay leader of his congregation, an established environmental and water law expert, and a part-time professor in the Law School at Baylor University for decades. Before the pandemic, Walt and I tried to meet for lunch often, and I looked forward to the appearance of his periodic columns in the Saturday "religion" section of the *Austin American-Statesman*. What I had considered a "throwaway" part of the paper had become a surprisingly serious effort by the local paper to engage meaningfully with the role of religion and spirituality in the city and region.

In his newspaper columns and in his two recent books, Walt focuses at all times on Jesus's command that we "love one another." He urges us to live mindfully, intentionally, and authentically in every day of the only life that we have to live. But, in writings about the importance of daily life, Walt never uses the word "quotidian." For Walt, daily life is far from being boring, tedious, routine. Every new day is precious because each minute of that day is the only time of which we can be sure. Walt tells us that, if we live every day mindfully, actively, and inclusively, we unconsciously create a meaningful past full of experiences from which we can construct an authentic and responsible future. The result, hopefully, will be a life well lived.

Walt goes beyond the currently fashionable emphasis on living "mindfully," which too often becomes but another form of self-absorption. Instead, he urges us simply to be responsibly "present" and connected to all that surrounds us—to nature, to those in our care and trust, and to all others who are in need. He draws on his own experiences as a husband, father, student, teacher, and friend as well as writings from both believers and non-believers. His "good news" is inclusive and expansive. And, in these troubled days, it could not be timelier. His voice, always irenic, is in his first book, *The Daily Practice of Life*, essentially pastoral. In *Authentic Living in All Seasons*, that voice appropriately becomes more prophetic, as befits the dark days in which it was written.

As I read Walt's writing over the past decade or so, my mind regularly turned to the Psalms. In Psalm 46:10 we are told to "Be still and know that I am God." Walt Shelton knows how to be still without becoming inert. He wants us to be familiar with our internal landscape without forgetting that outside of us is a world in desperate need. Even if we do not believe in the God of the Judeo-Christian tradition, or in any deity, we all need to learn to "be still." Walt tells us that all true "knowing" begins with "being still," that knowing oneself is the necessary precondition to authentic witness and service to those around us. Not until we know ourselves can we discern and faithfully discharge our responsibilities for others.

Particularly in *Authentic Living in All Seasons*, Walt's recurring focus on the crucial importance of loving and living in the moment called to my mind a passage from Henri-Frederic Amiel, a nineteenth century Swiss moral philosopher, essayist, and poet. Late in his tragically short life, Amiel, just as Walt does now, urgently reminded his reader of the importance of acting in the present moment: "Life is short, my friends, and we have but little time to gladden the hearts of those who journey with us. So be quick to love. And make haste to be kind."

Robert Walton Shelton is one of the finest human beings I have ever known. He is no longer my student; he is my friend. And, of late, he has become one of my spiritual guides, my mentor. I hope that you will now follow him in this book as he meditates on ways to "be still and know" as preparation for leading an authentic, intentional, and responsible life. You are in good hands.

Howard Miller
University Distinguished Professor Emeritus
Departments of History and Religious Studies
The University of Texas at Austin

Preface

We all have one opportunity to live. Regardless of religion, politics, race, gender-orientation, or other categorization, we all share one characteristic: mortality. The *length* of our present lives, whatever our perspective on any afterlife, varies with degrees of uncertainty. Although statistics and lifestyle choices might provide some insight to predict our longevity, no one possesses any guaranteed number of days. Life is uncertain beyond the present moment.

Therefore, how should we endeavor to live each day? What are our priorities and objectives at any given point in life? What are our sources for such concerns? Who are our mentors and role models? Do we identify with and participate in any faith-related or other communities that affect our personal flesh-and-blood journeys? By and large, what *choices* do we intend, make, and live daily—and why? What footprint, legacy, and memories will ultimately result in significance for our family, friends, community, and others?

In my first book, *The Daily Practice of Life: Practical Reflections Toward Meaningful Living* (CrossLink Publishing 2020), I emphasized that my priority as a Christian is endeavoring to follow the life-model and teachings of Jesus from a love-centered, inclusive, and pursuit-of-justice perspective. Rooted in personal experiences and consideration of the primary teachings of Jesus, as well as some teachings from other faith traditions, my intention was to present Jesus as *the* model not only for Christians, but also for anyone interested in living a meaningful life. Jesus's teachings of love, compassion, humility, integrity, inclusivity, and actively seeking justice and equal treatment for all pertains not only historically, but in the now as well. For Christians and all people, what matters are our intentions and active choices every single day. Doctrinal particulars are overrated. The key is how we live and how we treat others. As Jesus said so many times: "*Follow* me" (e.g., Mark 1:17, emphasis added). When we fall as we seek to walk this "narrow" and "hard" path of authentic "life" (see, e.g., Matt. 7:14), we should get up and start with fresh intention the next day, or better yet, the very next moment.

"Following" and living in a meaningful manner is *very hard work*. We will never reach 100% perfection, but that should be our daily objective. Jesus tells us in the Sermon on the Mount (Matt. 5–7), the largest collection of his teachings in the New Testament Gospels: "Be perfect . . ." (Matt. 5:48). He intended this as our aspirational goal in life and in each day that we live it. Intentionally striving to follow his path, model, and teachings is not simply something to want to do, casually. We should strive to be aware of our intentions, and willing to put effort into realizing them. We must be *fully committed and focused* on walking his path sincerely, both in good as well as challenging times. Each time we stumble along the way, we must rise up completely and recommit our intention to try harder. This is true repentance: a complete "turning" around to travel in the right direction. As a practical matter, aspiring toward human perfection demands all-out, consistent, non-wavering, and never-ending commitment. Essentially, we covenant for all this life to do our absolute best with God's and our fellow travelers' help and companionship.

A life of Christian faith, which is often consistent with other authentic faith traditions, has many components, including belief, creedal affirmation, doctrinal positions, prayer, meditative practice, community, and knowledge-based wisdom gained from teachers and personal experiences. Above all, however, our choices and how we consistently live are most important in our varied and limited years on earth. Good, informed choices and actions should be our top priorities as people of any faith or belief.

I have divided this book into two parts. Part I highlights three key elements of a satisfying and meaningful life that potentially shines a light for others and provides a positive legacy:

1. Focusing on the moment with full attention and awareness each day;
2. Dealing with the normal emotion of fear without letting the state of fear incapacitate us and prevent us from living intentionally and pursuing our goals; and
3. Identifying, refining, balancing, and living out our priorities.

Of these three, the first is most important, so it demands the most attention. Engaging in the hard work toward paying full and focused attention to individuals and circumstances in each moment of each day is the doorway to a life filled with practical acts of kindness and true love of others, which itself is the true path of an authentic and meaningful life.

Part II consists of twenty short chapters, which build on my collection of forty reflections in my first book. Most of these chapters are revisions to articles related to faith and life quality published in the *Austin American-Statesman* over the last three years. Many of the chapters draw in part on learning from personal experience, which might be the most underrated aspect of faith-based and other foundations for living a meaningful life. Many readers of my first book shared with me that they applied the individual chapters as daily "devotional"-type readings. Some might choose to use the chapters of Part II of this book in the same way—for reflection, including what you have learned from your own personal experiences, similar and otherwise.

I also include two appendices with more information on the religious roots of and certain clinical observations related to mindfulness (Appendix 1) and on developing new habits toward the goal of focused daily living (Appendix 2). The appendices have consecutive and traditional footnotes. In contrast, I used informal textual citations, noting the sources of brief quotations without pinpoint cites (other than biblical cites) or footnotes. I prefer this approach for smoother textual reading.

You will notice intentionally recurring themes, emphases, sources, and other similarities throughout the book. In my experience, we should always drive home major priorities for living, consistently reminding ourselves of their significance.

I am so glad you have chosen to read my book. I wish you all the best in your life journey.

Regarding the book cover, I took this picture (as I did for my first book) as representative of the book's contents. The still waters, colorful trees, and strong mountains reflect the beauty, tranquility, and peacefulness of a focused mind, overcoming harmful fear, and balanced priorities. The cabin in the distance at the water's edge embodies the stable home that we should work for and progress toward in our authentic faith and life journeys.

Walt Shelton, 2022

PART I

FOCUSED, FEARLESS, and BALANCED LIVING

Chapter 1

Key Components of Qualitative Living

If you had to identify just a few keys to living a meaningful life, what would you select? As intimidating as the inquiry and exercise appears, this formative introspective process can result in positive changes. It requires prayerfully and meditatively taking a hard, retrospective look at your life experiences relative to your priorities. For many, it might include re-examining and freshly evaluating one's choices, goals, and true priorities in life. What have our personal life experiences and observations of others' lives taught us about the true core aspects of living a life that matters? Is it one that will result, after we die, in a legacy and immortality of sorts, resulting from the imprint we left in our life circles?

Through personal, self-critical analysis, if we can boil it down to just a few key things that impact our ability to live as we intend, then we will have a way to transform for the better. This will afford us simple focal points to keep in the forefront of our minds for the rest of our days. We might also find that this life audit technique of looking inward is necessary periodically in order to refine our perspective as we face new challenges and circumstances. It can remind us of what we truly value and should actually practice daily to enhance the quality of not only our lives, but all the lives we are privileged to touch and influence.

As a Christian, I start with the teachings and life-model of Jesus as my guide. For me, this includes reading, reflecting upon, and seeking to integrate into my life the primary themes of the New Testament, especially within the Gospels and consistent with Jesus's Jewish heritage. This study and practice provide me with a list of what I term "character traits" that I want to actively live out. These life components are inclusively oriented and fit the pattern of other authentic faith traditions as well as simply helping to live a meaningful and impactful (morally and ethically) life as a decent human being.

A few passages in the New Testament sum up the most important core traits that we should aspire to live by habitually. Colossians 3:12–15 provides an especially stellar list: compassion, kindness, humility, gentleness, patience, forgiveness, love, harmony, peace, and thankfulness. What an incredible collection for active day-to-day living and relationships. For a Christian, living out these intentions means living "a life worthy" of following Jesus, as the apostle Paul "beg[s]" his readers (and us today as authentic followers of Jesus) to do (Eph. 4:1). Paul follows his injunction with a godly catalogue of virtues much like the Colossians list: humility, gentleness, patience, love, unity, and peace (Eph. 4:2–3). For anyone, Christian or otherwise, instilling these habits in intention and action results in a life that is a model of excellence and a prime example for others.

Being a great example to other people is like shining a bright light. Jesus told his followers in the Sermon on the Mount (Matt. 5–7) that they (and we) are "the light of the world," we should indeed, "let [our] light shine" for all to see, and we should never hide the luminosity of righteous and ethical living (Matt. 5:14–16). As a result, by making good choices, we can be both mentors and mentees, as well as role models, to one another.

What might we add to the aspirational habits that Paul emphasizes in Colossians and Ephesians to live as the brightest lights possible consistent with these ideals? The pursuit of justice includes caring in a special way for the poor, sick, oppressed, and others who are disadvantaged in any way—those who desperately need our help and do not stand much of a chance in life without it.

One of the most formative passages in the entirety of the Bible, found in the Gospel of Luke, includes an account of Jesus coming out of his time of introspection and bedevilment. While in the wilderness, he wrestled with his vocation and calling in life. In Luke 4:18–19, drawing on the book of Isaiah from his Jewish scriptural tradition, Jesus clearly stated: "The Spirit of the Lord is upon me, because he has anointed me to bring good news to the poor. He has sent me to proclaim release to the captives and recovery of sight to the blind, to let the oppressed go free."

In a similar vein within the Parable of the Great Judgment in Matthew 25, Jesus places the highest practical priority on feeding the hungry, giving a drink to the thirsty, welcoming the stranger, clothing the naked, taking care of the sick, and visiting prisoners (Matt. 25:34–36). These and similar acts of pure kindness are all things we can do frequently. It's as simple as picking one, opening our eyes and ears, and paying attention to the opportunities around us each day. More than anything, the daily pursuit of justice through practical acts of caring for those in need is important for Christians and anyone committed to living meaningfully. This is truly *love*.

PRACTICAL IMPLEMENTATION

So, what are some effective mechanisms and strategies to implement these fundamental goals and objectives both practically and actively for a life well-lived? In my experience, and in an effort to create a short list that I can remember each day, four prominent things stand out:

1. *Focusing on the present moment* with full awareness of opportunities;
2. *Not allowing being afraid to inhibit* us from moral and ethical living;
3. *Balancing our priorities* in life and finding ways to hit the "reset" button;
4. *Following through with altered living* when we sense that we are straying and out of balance.

The next three chapters of Part I focus on critical life-quality enhancing elements. As I noted in the Preface, the first is most important: focusing on the present, otherwise known as "mindfulness." This essential criterion for a meaningful life feeds the other two focal points, namely, effectively dealing with fear and engaging in the diligence to identify, periodically confirm or change, and balance our priorities. All these elements require the discipline of astute focus and attentiveness.

The remainder of this chapter highlights some major challenges of our current culture, as well as personal anecdotes of struggling though my own life to improve my "batting average" for living in the way I aspire to. I hope to encourage you to think through your own journey and experiences in such a way that will help you to understand yourself better; know when to give yourself a break; and determine how to do the best you can to make important changes in your daily actions.

SEASONS OF LIFE

Each "season" of our lives presents different challenges. For persons overwhelmed with work or other responsibilities that present seemingly insurmountable challenges, it is easy for day-to-day life to degrade into an intolerable burden. This is true for everyone, including people in traditional work environments, full-time parents with significant personal interests, retirees with a proliferation of time-filling activities, and anyone else who senses the headache-inducing pressure that there is just not enough time in each day.

The contemporary proliferation and infiltration of communication tools and methodologies compel many people to stay almost endlessly connected. Constantly staying in touch with work contacts, friends, extended family members, and even strangers becomes an expectation that feels like our "master." This mode of living has "sped up" our daily pace well beyond any reasonable comfort zone, forcing us toward multitasking as the norm, and negatively impacting both our health and our enjoyment of life.

Modern communication modes certainly offer benefits to enhance our days, such as staying in closer touch with loved ones, assisting in emergency situations, and offering potential efficiency in our work. Yet, it is easy for any of us to slip into the full-on oppression of 24/7 constant availability in the workplace or other potentially stressful contexts at any period in our lives. This wrings the joy and balance out of life compared to simplified and more easily paced days. Before we know it, the things we intended to be our priorities slip out of focus. Our fancy tools to stay in touch don't seem so "smart" anymore!

Within these contemporary circumstances of hyper-availability and trying to do too many things at once, the spring of 2020 initiated a "game changer" for everyone. The onset and longevity of the Coronavirus (COVID-19, "COVID") pandemic impacted all aspects of our professional and personal lives. Essentially, COVID ushered in an unexpected and most unwelcome season of life for everyone. COVID continues to complicate and degrade our lives, presenting uncertainties and challenges still going forward at the time of this writing. What strategies and habits can help us in this and other tough and uncertain periods? When things seemingly return to "normal," will we be able to take the best of what we learned and how we changed to augment the quality and pace of daily living moving forward?

Paying mindful attention, avoiding fearful stagnation, and engaging in periodic self-examination toward actualizing and balancing life priorities are important and potentially life-changing strategies toward a meaningful and satisfying existence. In extreme contexts, we might discover needed modifications of our life contexts. First and foremost, we may need intentional alterations in our perspective that will allow us to find a more focused and determined "practice" of living consistent with our priorities.

I hope my noted objectives, suggestions, and comments are beneficial in exacting times, such as but not limited to the COVID pandemic (which started before I wrote this book). More importantly, however, I hope they apply and can help us in *all* seasons of life.

Without question, the ever-increasing modes, speed, and efficiency of communication and related transmission of information enhance the stress of modern life. This was true before the pandemic, has intensified during it, and will continue with us after we emerge from COVID-related issues.

The ever-increasing and changing expectations of quick-response communication are formative, challenging, and exhausting. Nevertheless, one thing has not changed. As authentic human beings with the gift of one mortal life, we should sense and develop an ethical imperative to pay attention to each day, embrace the people and things we love most, and work hard to balance the personal and work dimensions of our lives in order to flood them and the people around us with authentic, meaningful daily living. Although the particulars of our lives differ, we should all endeavor to fully attain these objectives to the best of our efforts and abilities.

The ever-changing communicative, personal, social, and professional contexts for actualizing our higher calling for a meaningful and fulfilling day-to-day life, however, ultimately make that calling more difficult to achieve. On a broader and more significant qualitative scale, we are now challenged more than ever to balance work demands, including the potential for constant availability, with family and other personal priorities and interests.

CHOICES—IT'S UP TO US

Despite these challenges, something else at the very core of our humanity has remained constant over time: We are still free to *make our own choices* regarding *how* we endeavor to live. A helpful process is to periodically and intentionally think through and truly reassess how we are living day-to-day relative to our priorities in life—our "work" priorities as well as all aspects of our personal lives. Deliberately struggling through such a process can lead to positive and healthy changes. Engaging in this "personal audit" may result in increased contentment and enhanced competence in our respective "workplaces," whether those are found in traditional careers, our homes, in retirement, or otherwise. In most cases, we can choose our individual paths in life and circumstances that are conducive to consistently living out our preferences. In some contexts, our possibilities for change might include altering current settings and responsibilities. Extreme circumstances might trigger a more substantial change, such as moving to a different work or life setting, regardless of the expectations (real or imagined) of others or even ourselves.

The following chapters of Part I include some ideas that might help us cope better with the collective challenges and personal difficulties of modern living, touching on faith-related and ethical life practices as well as day-to-day quality of life. My comments, suggestions, and ideas relate to a few considerations toward living a full and authentic life in a high-quality, satisfactory, and rewarding manner. As noted previously, these aspects include: (1) staying focused and attentive to each part of our day (instead of wandering in dispersed and scattered thought and action) by practicing and developing habits toward mindfulness; (2) dealing with the inevitable fears of the modern world, including what feels like twenty-four-hour availability and expectations to accomplish an endless list of daily "to do" items; and (3) faithfully endeavoring to identify and intentionally live out our respective priorities in life, even if they point toward significant lifestyle changes.

PART OF MY STORY

What qualifies me to offer comments and potential input on such important matters as balancing personal life toward an improved experience? I sincerely care about living qualitatively in line with personal objectives, including putting in the hard work of developing ways to progressively attain such a lofty goal. For me, this is part of an authentic faith journey as a Christian—much like any person committed to another tradition, or someone simply committed to being a decent human being—one intent on modeling and then leaving a positive imprint in the one gift of life we all share. Additionally, I have struggled with balancing priorities and responsibilities over the years. I continue to dig deeply into my own issues to better understand them and implement helpful changes in my life. Although I regress at times, I endeavor to make progress in focused and balanced day-to-day living along with periodic reassessment of priorities. I experience an upgrade in my personal quality of life and experiences when I periodically engage in a life audit.

Within a variety of circumstances in my life, I can readily relate to consistently having way too much to do within a stressful atmosphere, as well as feeling a compulsion toward unrealistic expectations, self-imposed and otherwise. Further and more significantly, I empathize from experience with struggles related to priorities, including my family, health, rest, and personal interests. As I put all this together, I can identify the related exhaustion, periodic considerations of changing environments and habits, and the seemingly overwhelming changes needed in order to implement and better live out my life objectives. I believe that we can positively change our circumstances without compromising (while hopefully improving) qualitative and satisfying daily experiences that are more meaningful personally both for us and others—as well as rewarding and enjoyable.

Allow me to demonstrate this point using personal experience. Many of my "crunched life" personal experiences started in law school. I was a few months shy of thirty-one years old and had been married almost ten years (we hit forty-three years in May 2021) when I started law school. We also had two children (ages four and five) and a mortgage when I walked into my first class, Civil Procedure, as a 1L. I had a stable and relatively high-paying job that I left to attend law school. In fact, I made more money annually my last few years before law school than I did during my first few years at a large, prestigious law firm post-law school graduation. I needed to succeed academically, but I also had family-related obligations and priorities at that time, which I refused to put on hold. Although I was a full-time law student, I worked part-time my first two years, coached my son's soccer team, and did all I could to prioritize my family while doing my best to excel as a student who increased the average age of the student body.

I attempted to maintain numerous priorities through trial and error during law school. My efforts overwhelmed me at times. Yet, I approached it as a temporary season of overload in life with a purpose and an end date, all made possible by my family's strong support and encouragement. After law school, however, the daily combination of too much to do in too little time continued in an unhealthy manner beyond the school-defined, short-term season. My failure to slow down resulted in a fractured and unsatisfactory whole.

After graduation, I was fortunate to work within a very well-respected environmental law practice group at a large firm. What was meant to be a one-time opportunity to teach environmental law at Baylor Law School eventually complicated this excellent practice experience. Instead, the Baylor opportunity morphed into a thirty-plus-year and counting teaching career, technically part-time but now practically my full-time vocation.

About six years into practicing law and teaching, I hit the high point (i.e., personal low point) of overload, stress, and expectations. While working unreasonable hours as an attorney, I spent every Monday one hundred miles from home, teaching two three-hour environmental courses (one at a time) year-round on a quarter system. I prepared my teaching curriculum each weekend, tried to be a good dad and husband, led a faith-related discussion group once a week, and attempted to keep my daily running habit alive. On my teaching days, I spent an absurd amount of time on my old-style, first-generation cell phone (the size and weight of a brick), much of it on the road (pre-Bluetooth technology), related to law practice. The rest of the week, in addition to working in my office in Austin, I averaged one or two day trips a week via Southwest Airlines to Houston or Dallas for work. Additionally at that time, my mother in Tyler, Texas learned she had cancer and survived eleven months post-diagnosis. For the last several months of her life, I made day trips to Tyler from Austin (more than four hours one way in those 55 mph speed limit days) to spend time with her most Sunday afternoons. Personal side effects materialized in more stress, worry, and sciatica.

Within these circumstances, which in retrospect made me feel more like "Super-Type A" instead of Superman, I progressively identified and analyzed my choices and habits related to my intended priorities (mostly family and health). I realized I had to make changes. Although I procrastinated too long in transitioning to an improved and more rational work life, a tipping point caused imperative action to change. In a packed Love Field terminal in Dallas late one Friday afternoon, after yet another exhausting week culminating in a work-jammed day trip, something startling and unexpected finally and fully woke me up. I wanted so bad just to be at home with my favorite people, my wife and children (and dog). As I waited for my flight to board, I heard my name paged over multiple airport speakers. That was a first for me. With people jammed against me (no social distancing then), all of them also yearning to be homeward bound, I meandered to the nearest phone. That is how I learned my mother died: on a phone in a crowded, stress-filled airport with people rushing all around me. Amidst some tears and additional life auditing on the flight home, with the woman seated next to me moving further away, I decided to make several changes toward simplifying and enhancing my quality of life. A life that focused more on my family, health, and teaching (which I truly love as my vocation and primary work life) topped my short list.

I include the foregoing autobiographical information to provide examples of relevant experience with issues covered in Part I. First, it colors and perhaps explains to a certain extent my current perspective on these topics. Second, it illustrates why I believe we should meditatively consider and periodically reflect on our unique life experiences as authentic sources of learning and wisdom in relation to how we personally work and live going forward. I encourage anyone to do the same.

CHAPTER 2

Mindfulness: Focused Attention on Now

"The eye is the lamp of the body. So, if your eye is healthy, your whole body will be full of light; but if your eye is unhealthy, your whole body will be full of darkness."
Matthew 6:22–23a

". . . teach us to count our days that we may gain a wise heart."
Psalm 90:12

"Be careful . . . how you live, not as unwise people but as wise, making the most of the time."
Ephesians 5:15–16a

ONE THING AT A TIME—A NECESSITY

I was sitting in a crowded room with close to two hundred people with a shared and full table in front of me. I loaded my part of the table with my iPad, iPhone, the morning sports section of the San Antonio paper, a huge notebook full of substantive papers and speakers' bios, a legal pad, and a few pens, with a Redweld file at my feet full of notes on active work projects. Then I asked myself: "What am I doing?" Well, I was reading the sports pages, skimming the current speaker's paper and bio, rating the former speaker on a form, constantly glancing at my phone and iPad for indications of calls and messages, and drafting a fresh "to do" list. Many people refer to this as a necessary professional skill: multitasking. It occurred to me, however, to be problematic dispersion.

A few questions occurred to me: How many things can I do at a time? How many can I do well? It was as if I had come to a point where multitasking was the unchallenged and automatic default norm. Indeed, doing as much as possible is an inherent part of our culture and "feels" like a necessity, regardless of whether we are overly busy professionals, stay-at-home parents, retirees, or at any other station of life. Stopping to think about the two questions above is an uncommon skill to develop. Yet, when we take a deep, hard look at them as I did that day at my continuing legal education conference, my realization was obvious.

We can only do one thing well at a time. Otherwise, we are unfocused, distracted, and not at our *very best*. Qualitative activity, including work and every aspect of our lives, results from singular attention in the moment to the task or person in front of us. Sequential living instead of simultaneously trying to do as much as possible—doing one thing at a time with our full attention—is what mindfulness is all about. Conceptually, full and focused daily living is simple. In effective practice, however, it is a deliberate, intentional, hard-working, challenging, and lifelong process taken one day at a time. Progressing toward a mindfully focused approach to life, however, is worth all of our dedication and intention.

As noted in Chapter 1, contemporary communication modes tend to compel many of us to stay endlessly connected, not just with work, but with most everyone and everything else within our life's realm. This rushed style of living has driven our daily activities beyond any reasonable or comfortable pace. Without us realizing it, a constant state of inattentive diversion is forced upon us as normative. What is the solution? Slowing down and changing our basic daily perception of and approach to life through consistent hard work toward the new, healthier habit of a focused existence.

JESUS AND MINDFULNESS

Jesus the man is a stellar example of mindfulness in what he taught and how he lived. One of my favorite teachings that pertains to laser focus in the present moment is the passage noted at the outset of this chapter (Matt. 6:22), in which Jesus emphasized a "healthy" eye as an imperative that fills our "whole body" with "light" (Jesus taught with such vivid imagery and symbolism). Our "eye" is our momentary focus and is only "healthy" when we give our full and undivided attention to one person, task, or thought at a time. This truly fills us with "light," and that enlightenment attends singular focus. In addition to enriching our own lives, it is important to note that such pure attentiveness makes us bright lights for others. Daily focus, before we know it, naturally transforms us into potential role models and mentors. Jesus also taught his followers, providing another example of how he intends for us to let our "light shine before others" in order that we may give "light to all" when they observe our "good works" (Matt. 5:15–16). As we stray from pure attentiveness to the present moment, however, darkness can set in, dimming our illuminating example because we are no longer at our best to help, care for, attend to, and appropriately respond to what is right before us in the moment.

When we read through the four New Testament Gospels and look for hints and indications of themes and patterns in how Jesus lived as a man in his time, several things clearly emerge

about his life, how he lived daily, and who and what he prioritized. He was without question a Jewish rabbi and an observant
Jew. In this capacity, he cut to the true heart, meaning, and intent of his Jewish tradition, opposing the extreme literalism and
rules-oriented approach of certain Jewish religious and political
leaders of his time.

While Jesus championed the poor, sick, and victims of injustice, some of these influential and self-important leaders oppressed such disadvantaged people. Ultimately, this clash within
his own religious tradition cost Jesus his life. Problems arose with
his enemies when Jesus routinely did good works on the Sabbath
day by helping the needy instead of stoically observing nitpicky
rules about not "working" in most any way on that special day.
For Jesus, the heart of the Sabbath—and of living on any other
day—was quite clear. As he asked his opponents before healing
a man on the Sabbath: "I ask you, is it lawful to do good or to do
harm on the Sabbath, to save life or destroy it?" (Luke 6:9). The
answer was obvious then and is so now. Loving others by doing
good is always the right way regardless of anyone's rules, including ones that have been historically associated with God in an in-
flexible and literal manner with complete disregard for context.

Jesus also relaxed certain Jewish regulatory dietary restrictions, including in circumstances connected to the Sabbath.
While some powerful Jewish leaders lorded antiquated rules and
restrictions over others, Jesus prioritized human needs. As Jesus
clearly indicated to his critics: "The Sabbath was made for humankind and not humankind for the Sabbath" (Mark 2:27).

Jesus was one of the most inclusive and justice-oriented people who ever lived. He understood the authentic heart of Judaism
(and now, via Jesus, Christianity) by emphasizing the two greatest commandments: "Love the Lord your God with all your heart,
and with all your soul, and with all your strength" and "Love your
neighbor as yourself" (Mark 12:30–31). Jesus declared that "there
is no other commandment greater than these" (Mark 12:31). He

essentially established these intertwined commandments as a filter of sorts, with love at the center of everything meaningful in life. The inherent connection between the commandments is that we demonstrate and practically implement our full love for and devotion to God by loving acts of kindness, compassion, and care for other people.

Jesus embodied this full commitment to others by associating with the poor and emphasizing that they were "blessed" in God's sight (Matt. 5:3). He also paid full and loving attention to the sick and outcasts of his time, including lepers (e.g., Mark 1:40–42), which some prominent leaders in his faith disdained because they erroneously viewed their plight as a sign of God's disfavor rather than sickness simply being a part of life. Jesus's followers also included many women (e.g., Luke 23:27), which stood out as a particular rarity in his generation's overtly misogynous culture.

Because Jesus was so committed to inclusiveness, he truly modeled mindfulness. He was one man with one lifetime on earth, with a reputation and a following based in part on his profound helping of others through healing and the meeting of their needs.

We can all identify with the multiplicity of suffering and need in our world. If we simply stay in our own neighborhoods and open our eyes—if we are willing to see—we will find an incredible amount of need. How will we respond? Sometimes, the proliferation of people in need can be so overwhelming that it leads to stagnation. How can we make a difference? The resulting attitude often translates to doing nothing. What did Jesus, who was stormed with demands due to his keen ability to help, show and teach us? We meet one need at a time, one person at a time.

One example of Jesus helping one person at a time is the account of the woman who had suffered serious bleeding for years. Mark tells us in his gospel that Jesus sensed power going out of him when the woman touched his clothing in the midst of a very large crowd. When he asked who touched him, his followers said the crowd was so large, how could they answer such a question? When the woman disclosed her actions and immediate healing, Jesus said her faith made her well and told her to go peacefully with healing (Mark 5:24b–34). Similarly, Jesus met a leper who sought him out one-on-one and chose to clear his disease with a touch (Mark 1:40–42).

We can learn a lot from these and other examples. Helping others happens one person and one need at a time. Often, the person needing help must seek the right person for assistance, and the one who helps must be willing to offer a focused "touch" of healing without being preoccupied by other matters.

In addition to doing all he could to care for one person at a time in a focused and sequential manner, Jesus was a fantastic storyteller. He used imagery to draw verbal pictures of everyday scenes (both in parables and otherwise) to drive home his emphases. The parable of the rich man and Lazarus in Luke 16:19–31 is an important and striking example. At first blush, this story does not seem to be about mindful focus. Yet, after deeper consideration, it informs us about what it means to truly "see" and respond to what is right before us daily.

Arguably, the story of the rich man and Lazarus is one of the most important parables in the New Testament. Notably, it is the only parable in which Jesus named a participant in the story: the poor man, "Lazarus." Although the rich man is sometimes referred to as "Dives," this is misleading because *dives* is simply the Latin word for "rich man." In this parable, Jesus describes Lazarus as completely destitute: poor, sick, hungry, and apparently homeless. In stark contrast, Jesus tells his followers that the rich man wore fine clothes, feasted sumptuously, and apparently lived in a gated estate. In the end, they both die. Jesus describes a role reversal in the afterlife, with Lazarus eternally comforted in a heavenly existence and the man who had everything and everyone at his disposal in his mortal life in constant agony in the flames of Hades.

This, as with other parables, is not a prophecy of the afterlife. Rather, parables tend to have a central message or two within the context of a story or anecdote, which was often familiar to the audience. The role of the afterlife dichotomy is to highlight the central importance of how we live relative to people in need.

What does this have to do with mindfulness and a divine, present-moment focus? Notably, Jesus did not even hint that the rich man was overtly cruel or actively harmed poor Lazarus. Rather, the implication is that the rich man *failed to even notice* Lazarus. The rich man had an "unhealthy eye" by failing to see the need right in front of him every day as he left home. I imagine the rich man planning out his business day and thinking of a multiplicity of opportunities for himself as he left his extravagant home each morning, never truly seeing Lazarus and *only Lazarus* in the moment as he walked by him. The rich man failed to focus and respond by helping to meet another person's basic needs. The rich man's mind and attention were fractured and dispersed, too multifaceted to truly "see" with an opportunity to be full of true "light." He was distracted from the present, which means he was miles from being mindful. This reminds me of what the author of the book of James says about the "rich," that "in the midst of a busy life, they will wither away" (James 1:11b).

One other aspect of the parable deserves our attention: when the rich man in Hades asks Abraham to send someone to warn his brothers. One can assume that, like the rich man, the brothers' approach to enrichment neglected by omission people in obvious need. Abraham, speaking from heaven, simply says that the brothers need only "listen" to "Moses and the prophets" (Luke 16:29). Remember that Judaism was the tradition of Jesus, which is the strong, connected root of Christianity. We should always keep in mind that the historical Jesus was an observant Jew and a Jewish rabbi, with followers who later became the first Christians.

Examples from Moses and the prophets (forming part of the Hebrew Bible and Christian Old Testament) that emphasize focusing one's loving and helpful attention on others abound. One stellar source of timeless nuggets is an important chapter in Leviticus, which is one of the books of Moses (the first five books of the Bible). Leviticus 19 is the ethical heart of the "Holiness Code" (Lev. 17–26). In this important and ancient biblical chapter, God speaks to Moses with some imperatives—applicable for all times—related to caring for those in need, as well as to exercising justice and equity. Verse 2 is the common predicate to these significant injunctions: "Speak to *all* the congregation . . . and say to them: You *shall be holy*, for I the Lord your God am holy" (Lev. 19:2, emphasis added). Thus, God's demands thousands of years ago—and cutting across generations ever since—relate to godliness, which makes sense because God created us "in his image . . . male and female . . . and blessed [us]" (Gen. 1:27–28a).

Holiness, another timeless imperative in the Holiness Code, means caring for the poor and for people who are different from us. Addressing farmers, God said, "When you reap the harvest of your land, you shall not reap to the very edges of your field . . . You shall not strip your vineyard bare, or gather the fallen grapes of your vineyard; *you shall leave them for the poor and the alien*" (Lev. 19:9–10, emphasis added). More generally, if we have more than we need, we must share with people who do not have enough. Further, God implored, "You shall not defraud your neighbor; you shall not steal; and you shall not keep for yourself the wages of a laborer until morning. You shall not revile the deaf or put a stumbling block before the blind" (Lev. 19:13–14a).

For all of us, holiness includes honesty and treating others fairly in a timely manner, especially when we are in a position of power or control over them. We must respect and help anyone who is disabled or otherwise impaired. Two final examples from the "holiest" chapter of the Holiness Code are the most important; they embody true godliness—or simply being the finest of people, which are one and the same. Through Moses, God demanded and still compels us all: "You shall not take vengeance or bear a grudge . . . but *you shall love your neighbor as yourself*" (Lev. 19:18, emphasis added), and, more expansively and strikingly: "When an alien resides with you in your land, you shall not oppress the alien. The alien who resides with you shall be to you as the citizen among you; *you shall love the alien as yourself*" (Lev. 19:33–34a, emphasis added). Thus, if we want to be like God (or the equivalent, i.e., the absolute best of human beings), we should actively love everyone, including people who differ from us or our affiliations.

How does being holy relate to mindfulness? We have no chance to approach holiness unless we focus our complete attention, with all our senses, on the moment, regardless of the person or task at hand. Returning to the Scriptures quoted at the outset of this chapter, Psalm 90 and Ephesians 5 speak to me of the necessity of daily focus and of the need for striving to *practice* mindfulness in how we live. The psalmist prayerfully asks God to "teach us to count our days that we may gain a wise heart" (Ps. 90:12). We count our days by living them one at a time, resulting in a unique and centered wisdom through experience of how we should qualitatively live. Likewise, Paul wisely counseled his friends in Ephesus to be "careful . . . in how you live, not as unwise people but as wise, making the most of the time" (Eph. 5:15–16a).

Living with full presence in each "now" requires the utmost intention and care. Recognizing our mortality, with any day potentially being the last of our limited time, reinforces the urgency of working toward the daily practice of staying attentive. As a daily prayer (maybe several times a day), we might take a deep breath and say, "God, please give me eyes of singleness, not multiplicity."

CHAPTER 3

Avoiding The Stagnation of "Being Afraid"

How does fear factor into and affect the practice of authentically living? In a larger and more significant context, how does fear impact relationships with our families and friends, as well as our health, needed rest, and other parts of life? Fear's impact on our obligations and its integration into all aspects of our lives are not often addressed, thought about, or understood.

For the purposes of this section, it is helpful for us to distinguish at the outset between feeling fear and what I will characterize as *being* afraid." Fear as an emotion is a normal and often helpful aspect of being human. For example, such a feeling can keep us from running into a burning building, walking across a busy highway, or taking on projects in areas wholly outside of our expertise and experience.

The condition of "being afraid" is different. By this, I mean a hesitant condition that can result in an almost immovable state, where we are so petrified that we produce nothing or very little of value. Unexpected or unrealistically demanding circumstances can augment fear into this immobile condition. For example, an unexpected worldwide pandemic, overload of work projects or family obligations, and speed-of-light communication avenues coupled with unrealistic presumptions for availability, response, and performance can trigger this negative state of mind. The petrifying *fear of making a mistake* is among the biggest potential challenges for busy, contemporary professionals, parents, and others. Another fear shared by many is that of not readily knowing the answer to every question. This is accompanied by feeling like we should be able to immediately and fully answer all questions within our substantive areas of expertise or experience-based knowledge. Both manifestations of fear—of mistakes or of lack of expected personal knowledge—can cause enormous stress sensations. Neither is conducive to a qualitative daily life. At an extreme, such apprehensions contribute to a sense of ineptitude and lack of productivity, which can degrade our work, self-image, health, and lives. This is especially true of an ongoing and overshadowing attitudinal fear of making a mistake.

So, what can we do about fear inhibiting our daily performance and quality of life? Let's start by giving ourselves a break! We should remember that, regardless of our perceived level of experience and sophistication in certain areas (whether by ourselves or others), we are human. As humans, every one of us is subject to imperfection.

We want to strive for perfection; however, improvements along the path toward this worthy objective do not effectively occur without mistakes and other stumbles along the road of learning. With proper reflection, guidance from mentors and role models, and appropriate response actions, our mistakes are often our best opportunities for positive change going forward.

We should always yearn for our words of advice and the examples we set to be as correct and helpful as possible, which almost always involves taking our time to truly focus on each day's relevant opportunities and issues. Nevertheless, we should always be ready and willing to say, "I don't know," and sometimes add, "Let me look into it, consider it further, and follow up with you." When we do make a mistake, the usual best remedy is to admit and correct it in a timely manner. This sets an excellent example of humility and helpfulness and provides the opportunity for us to close a loop on known errors of a professional, or more importantly, a personal nature.

As a practical matter, have you noticed that the more you learn about something (such as your major in college or area of expertise in your work), the more you realize how much you *don't* know? Over my years practicing and teaching environmental law, I felt progressively overwhelmed by the expanse of each area of the subject matter and the complexity of seemingly endless issues. Pretending to know a great deal about something often signals an elementary understanding, or worse yet, an intolerable degree of arrogance.

Over the years, I have often suggested to my law students that they should always be ready to answer any client or anyone else with, "I don't know." These are three of the wisest words anyone can speak. Personally, I do not want to associate or spend much time with anyone who pretends or gives the appearance of immediately knowing the answer to almost *any* inquiry. Again, when we do make a mistake, the remedy is often to admit and correct it in a timely manner.

Drawing again on faith-related roots, Rabbi Harold Kushner has some very helpful input on coping with fear in his book, *Conquering Fear: Living Boldly in an Uncertain World* (Anchor Books 2010). His subtitle is an excellent slogan for working toward a better, healthier, more balanced combination of priorities within the demands and often unattainable expectations associated with modern life.

I am a huge fan of Rabbi Kushner and his practical, life-experience-based writings. His audience for some of his books should consist in part of inclusively minded Jewish readers, as well as *anyone* (faith tradition or not) interested in living a meaningful life. One of my favorite Kushner quotes is his suggestion in

When All You've Ever Wanted Isn't Enough (Pocket Books 1986) to "fill each day with one day's worth of meaning." He is a prolific writer and best known for his first book, *When Bad Things Happen to Good People* (Avon Books 1981). Rabbi Kushner wrote this book after the premature death of his son at age fourteen of a rare and arbitrary disease, emphasizing that we find goodness in the loving and caring response of others to tragedy. Based on what he has endured, as well as the decades during which he has counseled people as a rabbi and chaplain in the military, Kushner has "standing" to authentically comment upon real-life issues and provide legitimate input for others. In utilizing the legal terminology "standing," I mean that a person's life circumstances *qualify* them through experience to provide comments and suggestions for others. That is one of my criteria for considering the counsel of certain authors and speakers.

In *Conquering Fear*, Rabbi Kushner counsels: "Our goal should not be the total absence of fear but the mastery of fear, being the master of our emotions rather than their slave. Our goal should be to recognize legitimate fears, dismiss exaggerated fears, and not let fear keep us from doing the things we [want or are reasonably expected] to do."

In a similar vein, Kushner suggests that "[o]ur goal should never be denial of fear but the mastery of fear, *the refusal to let fear keep us from living fully and happily*" (emphasis added). We could add that recognizing, facing, and controlling fear can help us reasonably *pace* ourselves so that we can enjoyably and qualitatively perform to the best of our ability within all of our life priorities.

Alexi Pappas is a professional athlete, filmmaker, actress, and an amazing writer. She represented Greece in the 2016 Olympics and ran in the 10,000-meter finals, which is the longest race on the track in the Olympics. She loads her raw and revealing memoir, *Bravey* (The Dial Press 2021), with an open and integrity-based wisdom resulting from tumultuous ups and downs in her life, from the height of running in the Olympics to a serious, multiyear battle with clinical depression. I utilize Pappas's book in the final chapter (or devotional) of Part II.

Pappas exudes confidence and "standing" to articulate life-altering insights for anyone interested in improving their quality of life. These are based on her own life experiences, her observations of others, the advice of life-giving mentors, medical professionals, and devoted family members and friends, and her intentional reflections.

In her chapter titled "Love," Pappas offers helpful insight to deal with fear in the context of encouraging her readers to believe in and intentionally pursue "potential." In telling the story of how she and her husband "braved" through anxious times to pursue what they wanted in life—namely, professional sports and filmmaking—when their contemporaries had traditional jobs and steady incomes, Pappas wisely suggests "focus[ing] on the path ahead rather than stress[ing] about the road not taken." Regarding that time in their lives, she emphasizes that "[a]nxiety crept in" and "confidence in their potential was . . . confronted by a new adversary: fear." Further, "being motivated by fear of failure is the surest way to fail [because] you become fueled by *desperation* rather than *passion*" (emphasis added).

Fear is a very personal issue—we all experience it. We must realize that feeling fear is a natural human emotion, yet there are generally two types of fear. Good, healthy fear protects us when it causes us not to act, such as not crossing a busy interstate highway on foot. However, there are times when we should evaluate whether a fear is unhealthy and then push through. Otherwise, unhealthy fears can potentially petrify and immobilize us, preventing us from pursuing our goals and dreams, or from simply doing our very best in a difficult situation.

Moving beyond bad fear takes willpower and courage, which is especially important when we have a strong sense of vocation or calling. As Pappas succinctly puts it, "the time to make up [our] mind[s] about what is possible is never."

Fortunately, when it comes to dealing with fear or any other tough hurdle in life, we are not alone. God is with us and comes in many forms, including family, the best of friends, counselors, mentors, and an abiding source of strength and peace.

CHAPTER 4

Balancing Life Priorities Through Periodic Self-Reflection

THE VALUE OF SELF REFLECTION

W hat are our priorities in life? How do we determine them and revisit them for analysis and potential change? How does our profession fit in as a priority—is it balanced and integrated with other predominant objectives in life? Can we become so obsessed with and driven by success, with all of its pressures, expectations, and time consumption, that we either never ask questions like these or simply become numb toward them? Perhaps we reach a threshold of hyper-attention to our work lives after which we feel trapped and unable to change.

I do not have all the answers to such questions, other than partially for myself within different seasons of my life, including the continuing COVID-19-driven period at the time of this writing. These and similar questions are important but personal. We might also discover that simple, periodic *awareness* and exploration of life-quality questions can be more important than fully answering them. Answers and ideas vary by individual and within the respective stages of life. We might benefit from periodically identifying these or similar personal questions and meditatively thinking through them in solitude. We could also consider talking through some of our questions and ideas with people we share our lives with, including other busy professionals we respect, and especially with mentors.

Negative consequences can flow from losing touch with what is truly important in one's life. This can happen to even the best of people.

LIFE AUDITS: PRIORITIZING OUR LIVES

Practicing life auditing is an excellent periodic exercise. Annual meditative self-examination is a good start. We might combine a personal "hard look" audit with a recurring time period, such as seasons rooted in religious tradition (e.g., utilizing Lent and Easter in Christianity or Rosh Hashanah and Yom Kippur in Judaism for our own solitary examination and potential changes). Alternatively, we could use other annual seasons for a fresh start, such as the fall when kids return to school and the trees change colors. Each New Year or birthday could be another reminder—assuming we work toward serious and meaningful New Year's resolutions after deliberately contemplating and analyzing our experiences during the prior year.

Life audits can include reflections on how we are spending our time relative to our intentions and to what really matters to us, as well as reaffirming and rethinking our personal priorities. This should include an ethically-based, high-standard professional or correlated "work" life *balanced* with our families, health, friends, and other important people and things. Without taking a fresh and honest look at our intentions in connection, and sometimes in contrast, with how we are spending our days, the time we have left might simply get away from us.

Life auditing can be an empty and unsatisfying experience if we are afraid and unwilling to change. We might discover that we are overly attached to a professional goal or objective, perhaps idyllic or dream-like, which is problematic and no longer feasible. In his book *Seasons in a Man's Life* (Ballantine Books 1978), Daniel Levinson addresses the potential realization of giving up or renouncing one's dream. This dream could be a higher position or other status in our career. Such an objective might no longer fit our life circumstances. It might drag us down. Worse yet, it could be a major cause of us not attending to more important aspects of life, as well as making us less effective in our current positions. In *When All You've Ever Wanted Isn't Enough*, Rabbi Kushner addresses this phenomenon. He calls "The Dream" the "vision we had when we were young[er] . . . that we would be somebody truly special." Our dream might relate more to our perception of *others* thinking we are someone special once we achieve apparent high-ranking status. Per Kushner, falling short of an objective after years of holding it in a vice-grip can make us "feel like failures." Additionally, Kushner states, "We will never be happy until we stop measuring our real-life achievements against that Dream."

In *Trauma Stewardship: An Everyday Guide to Caring for Self While Caring for Others* (Berrett-Koehler Publishers, Inc. 2009), Laura van Dernoot Lipsky encourages her readers to remember that "we have options at every step of our lives." She further advises that we all "choose our own path." Importantly, Ms. Lipsky adds, "We can make a difference without suffering; we can do meaningful work *in a way that works for us and for those we serve*" (emphasis added). When faced with overly challenging circumstances, we might decide to transition to new circumstances and surroundings. Ms. Lipsky reminds us, however, that, "Plan B does not need to be a completely different lifestyle; it can be as subtle as a change in our attitude and the way we approach our existing commitments."

Life changes, including those within a rough life-season, current work setting, or transition to a new job, are never easy. Yet, they are sometimes necessary for our own well-being as well as the well-being of those we assist, who will benefit from our new and improved outlook or changed circumstances because we can better attend to their best interests. According to Ms. Lipsky, "Many traditions teach us that regardless of anything external, we can create and recreate how we feel, view the world, and experience our surroundings simply by shifting our perspective." Tying into practicing mindfulness, she reminds us that we "can ask, 'Where am I putting my focus?'" As Viktor Frankl emphasizes in *Man's Search for Meaning* (Ilse Lasch trans., Beacon Press 2006, originally published in 1959), people are "not fully conditioned and determined . . . [but] ultimately [they are] self-determining." Further and more importantly, "Every human being has the freedom to change at any instant."

CONCLUSION

Most meaningful aspects of life involve hard work, which is continually in process and subject to refinement. This is especially true during difficult and unexpected times beyond our control. Striving toward full attention in each moment and relationship is among the noblest pursuits of all. Further, developing and following better habits can help us, in Rabbi Kushner's words noted above, to "fill each day with one day's worth of meaning," without paralysis by fear, and consistent with our priorities and intentions.

We must then wake up to a fresh start each morning intent upon doing the same thing, only better, than the day before. This helps us be better people in the context of a happier and more fulfilling life, in all seasons.

PART II

PRACTICAL REFLECTIONS AND MEDITATIONS

CHAPTER 1

Acceptance While Endeavoring to Change for the Better

The daily quality of my life changed a few years ago without expectation or warning with the abrupt onset of a rare muscular disorder. It includes varying degrees of pain and dysfunction unless I am asleep. Fortunately, my version is segmented, meaning it affects only one muscle group. It impairs but does not fully limit activities I enjoy. Further, the symptoms are treatable. I am progressively improving with great family and medical support. In fact, my symptoms (which require constant "work" on my part) have improved so much to be unnoticeable most days, but the daily effort wears me out by early evening. Thankfully, the condition is neither life threatening nor shortening. Unfortunately, however, there is no cure, and the chance of remission (always temporary) is close to zero.

Others certainly deal with more serious health issues. My heart goes out to them and to anyone struggling with disease. Nevertheless, mine has been a load for me. I expect the daily grind of dealing with the circumstances will stick with me. Unfortunately, I am a wimp when it comes to such struggles.

How do we accept painful realities in our own and others' lives—and in our world—while working hard and doing the best we can to effectuate positive changes? Regarding the storms we must pass through in life, Archbishop Desmond Tutu says, "We cannot succeed by denying what exists. The acceptance of reality is the only place from which change can begin." The Dalai Lama adds that "stress and anxiety come from our expectations of how life should be. When we can accept that life is how it is . . . we are able to ease the ride, to go from . . . suffering . . . to . . . greater ease, comfort, and happiness."

These words of wisdom from such prominent, humble, and inclusive world leaders of both Christianity (the archbishop) and Buddhism (the Dalai Lama) are from *The Book of Joy* (Avery/ Penguin Random House 2016) by Douglas Abrams, who is Jewish. He adds his own helpful insights throughout the book. Best read slowly, a few pages at a time in a devotional style so that the spiritual insights sink in, the book chronicles a week of meetings and discussions on various subjects that took place in 2015.

There is a lot more to learn about the Nobel Peace Prize-winning Archbishop Tutu and Dalai Lama, including their experiences with and responses to violence, oppression, and exile. For now, their words exchanged in these face-to-face meetings between friends are treasures indeed. They each advocate a wide perspective on life that primarily focuses on the needs of others and not taking ourselves too seriously (that includes a sense of humor) all while not neglecting our own personal issues.

Regarding suffering of any kind, these spiritual giants draw an important distinction between an immediate reaction and a pause to reflect and collect ourselves before making an appropriate response. In my personal experience over the last few years, I can readily identify the difference between slamming my fist against a door on a bad day (never a good idea, but fortunately, I never broke my hand) and pausing, breathing, and considering what I might continue doing to make things better. In the broader context of encountering hatred, injustice, or oppression, enacting a path of intentional pause, reflective consideration, and response may lead to a more compassionate, understanding, defusing, and effective change than a gut reaction.

In Abrams's chapter titled "Acceptance: The Only Place Where Change Can Begin," Abrams emphasizes that "[a]cceptance . . . is the opposite of resignation and defeat." Further from Abrams: "The kind of acceptance that the Dalai Lama and the Archbishop were advocating is not passive. It is powerful. It does not deny the importance of taking life seriously and working hard to change what needs changing, to redeem what needs redemption."

Whether we are talking about personal struggles with disease, social injustice, or any type of suffering, the point is to thoughtfully and *actively work* and do our very best toward positive change. Whether rooted in Buddhism, Judaism, or Christianity (the three prominent perspectives in *The Book of Joy*), another authentic faith tradition, or simply a keen sense of humanity, each of our lives is a gift. We should treasure and qualitatively enjoy them, and that includes working toward improvement in the face of any type of personal or social disease.

CHAPTER 2

Christians and Jewish Holy Days

Have you ever wondered why Christians do not constructively celebrate or pay serious attention to Jewish holy days and seasons? It makes no sense to me. Judaism is our root and was the religion of Jesus, a rabbi in his time. Most Christians I know (including me in the past) refer to and think of Jewish holy days as "Jewish holidays." Many Christians also consider their own holy days and seasons, such as Christmas, Lent, and Easter, from a holiday perspective. Instead, we should all consider digging deeply into their meanings and observances in order to reflect on and enhance our faith journeys. We can learn and experience even more by paying some attention to and learning something about the holiest days of other faith traditions.

I respect and understand that full observance, utilization, and immersion into Jewish holy seasons is for people of the Jewish faith. I also ask that if you are a Jewish reader of this chapter, please forgive my elementary knowledge and understanding of (but deepest respect for) your high holy days and season, Rosh Hashanah (Jewish New Year) and Yom Kippur (Day of Atonement).

My basic understanding is that the period incorporating the Jewish New Year and the Day of Atonement (which I will call the "season") involves numerous days of intense focus, reflection, meditative introspection, and repentance on the prior year as it relates to God's forgiveness, as well as our forgiveness of others and ourselves. Intertwined with this experience is a "freeing up" as we enter the year ahead, offering the potential for a morally and religiously transformed life through better choices and habits. The Day of Atonement is rooted in part in two passages from the book of Leviticus in the Hebrew Bible/Christian Old Testament: Leviticus 16:29–34 and 23:26–32. It is an especially holy sabbath of self-denial that involves prayer, fasting, and abstaining from work and certain pleasures.

What a wonderful annual practice and discipline. It is both a dynamic personal and communal experience of God's forgiveness for wrongdoing and, importantly, a prospective refocusing toward having a truly changed life. In my Christian tradition, I see a parallel to this authentic, faith-based experience of self-examination during the annual season of Lent leading up to Easter. Good Friday and Easter Sunday are the culmination of this period, emphasizing God's forgiveness, being dead to the past, and prospectively becoming alive to a new path: endeavoring as a new person to follow the life model and teachings of Jesus.

As a practical matter, each seasonal Jewish and Christian tradition encourages an annual religious and moral life audit of sorts, with the objective of emerging with better habits and renewed priorities in our lives.

In Rabbi Harold Kushner's recent book, *Echoes of Sinai* (Curtis Brown Studios 2018), which is a collection of his favorite sermons, he talks about Yom Kippur and actual life change. In the chapter and sermon titled "The Future Can Change the Past," he talks about the central concept of *teshuvah*. I have not studied or intensely investigated the roots or scope of *teshuvah*, but my understanding is that it involves change and is similar to repentance. Rabbi Kushner then describes the possibility of a strikingly effective change into a new person. He contrasts the meaning of *teshuvah* with "repentance" (how *teshuvah* is sometimes interpreted) and understands *teshuvah* as a richer concept of change. Similarly, Jewish scholar and historian Henry Abramson describes the Yom Kippur experience as a joyful time with an emphasis on "returning" to core principles of Jewish holiness.

For me, Kushner's and Abramson's descriptions of truly dramatic and ethically based changes in life coincide with my Christian perspective of what Jesus and John the Baptist before him meant by true, life-changing repentance. Jesus and John implored their listeners to fundamentally change, to live by a daily response action to God's love for us, because the kingdom of God was present then and is still here now. The ushering in of God's kingdom depends on how we all react to God's love, or if one prefers, simply to the profound gift of life.

Historically, the New Testament Gospels (e.g., Luke 2:41–42; John 7:10) indicate that Rabbi Jesus, his parents, and his initial followers (all Jewish) observed and participated in certain Jewish festivals and traditions during his lifetime. Whatever our terminology, our respective traditions emphasize the need for periodic self-examination followed by ethically based, consistent recommitment to authentic change in how we act. Finding common ground in our traditions—especially for Christians learning more about the most significant traditions of our Jewish heritage—can be a vehicle to enhancing actual positive changes in how we live daily. The same holds true of looking for common themes and practices with other faith traditions beyond our own, instead of emphasizing our differences, or worse yet, demonizing anyone who has a different belief system or perspective.

CHAPTER 3

Authentic Light in a New Year

As I emphasized in the preceding chapter and elsewhere in my writings, I strongly support and personally endeavor to practice periodic life auditing, which includes taking a *hard* look at how one has and is living relative to one's priorities in life. For many of us, our life priorities are grounded and heavily rooted in our faith. How do we intend to live day-to-day? Looking deep within, how do we grade our performance since our last introspective analysis? Do we need to make changes in our habits, such as incorporating a daily routine that includes needed reminders of what is important to us, so that we can live our lives authentically?

My chosen time for periodic examination is the beginning of each calendar year with the holiday season fully in the rearview mirror. For me, this fresh start works best as a process undertaken over several days (or even weeks) in order to examine my previous actions and make necessary alterations of my deeds so that my intentions and actions coincide. Perhaps most importantly, I typically realize my need for an attitude adjustment toward having more compassion and care for others, as well as expressing greater thankfulness for the gift of life and all that I am privileged to possess.

In some of these introspective times, I thematically focus on "light" and its importance in life. In my Christian tradition, Jesus taught his followers that "we are the light of the world" (Matt. 5:14). Instead of hiding it, we should let our "light shine before others, so that they may see [our] good works" (Matt. 5:16).

Two thousand years ago, what did Jesus the Jewish rabbi mean when he called his followers to be bright lights? How would Jesus practically link light to daily living in a Jewish tradition that he held in common with his contemporary followers?

The rich book of Isaiah in the Hebrew Bible and Christian Old Testament is key in considering this issue. The New Testament Gospels indicate that Jesus imprinted Isaiah's words in his mind. One of the most prominent examples of this is found in the Gospel of Luke. Chapters 3 and 4 of Luke include accounts of John the Baptist demanding repentance (meaning a changed life) of the crowd listening to him, as well as the account of John's baptism of Jesus, where Jesus emphatically sensed God saying, "You are my Son, the Beloved" (Luke 3:22).

Following this revelation, Jesus struggled with its implication for his earthy vocation during a season of temptation and self-reflection in the wilderness. He confidently emerged with a strong initial public message at the synagogue in Nazareth, quoting from the scroll of Isaiah: "The spirit of the Lord is upon me, because he has anointed me to bring good news to the poor. He has sent me to proclaim release to the captives and recovery of sight to the blind, to let the oppressed go free" (Luke 4:18, drawing from Isa. 61:1–2 and 58:6).

Jesus identified with Isaiah to a great extent. So, what might this tell us about living as "light" in the world as an objective for a qualitative-based life going forward? The emphases of such a life should include love, compassion, care, and the active pursuit of justice for people who are in need or oppressed in any way.

CHAPTER 4

How Should We Approach and Interpret the Bible?

66 **I**f the Bible says it, I believe it." I heard that definitive asser-
tion many times as a boy growing up in a conservative East
Texas church. People also repeatedly called the Bible "God's
Word" (singular), indicating it is all a person needs to know. These
often-well-intentioned descriptions sound nice and simple. They require no true learning or consideration of context. Further, they de-
mand very little, if any, personal thought or analysis in light of what
we experience and observe in our lives. Such rigidity discourages digging deeply into the Bible and its diverse books and parts in order to
think about, study, interpret, and beneficially apply the writing to our
lives. Worse yet, such inerrant, devoid-of-context approaches can in-
vite misuse and abuse, both spiritually and politically. An "inerrancy
without exception and with blinders on" approach to the Bible essentially makes the *Bible itself* God instead of a collection of books about
God and God-related matters, with different sources, from varying
times and a multitude of contexts.

When I started reading and thinking about the Bible in high
school, such narrow expressions about faith made no sense to
me. Now I see this "just open the Bible and take any piece of it as
literal and applicable right now" as a flawed approach. It invites

judgment, abuse, and misuse, and restricts one's view of God. Making the Bible itself into God seems like a form of idolatry.

The Bible is a rich, multi-faceted Judeo-Christian collection of very special, instructive, and inspirational books. Biblical books contain God's "words" through human writers over an expanse of time and relevant to a variety of differing historical and other contexts. These special books, as well as sacred writings in other traditions, can be a gateway and springboard toward starting to understand God and providing a foundation for living a meaningful life.

So, as a practical matter, how should we approach the Bible? As a Christian, I take my cue from Jesus. As a Jewish rabbi, his "Bible" was the Hebrew Bible, essentially the Christian Old Testament. I am not suggesting Christians change this traditional terminology, but we can also think of it as "Jesus's Bible." Technically, the Hebrew Bible did not come together in "canonized" form until a hundred years or so after Jesus died. However, Jews of his time accepted most all of it as authoritative scripture.

How did Jesus approach his Bible? The New Testament Gospels shed some helpful and informative light. For me, a few key aspects stand out: (1) Jesus studied it and listened inquisitively to experts; (2) he did not take all of it literally or out of context; (3) he prioritized certain parts and themes; and (4) he did not put a lid on learning or on the potential for God's continued revelation and inspiration in our lives.

The following are a few examples. First, Jesus began seriously studying the Bible early in his short life. The Gospel of Luke tells us that when Jesus was twelve years old, he stayed behind in Jerusalem after an annual trip with his family, as observant Jews, to Jerusalem for Passover (Luke 2:41–42). "After three days" searching for him, his parents "found him in the temple, sitting among the teachers, listening to them and asking questions" (v. 46). He was inquisitive and open to listening to experts about his Bible in his formative childhood.

Second, some prominent Jewish leaders of the day challenged Jesus about what to do with a woman caught in adultery. They pointed out that, "The law of Moses commanded us to stone [i.e., kill in a painful way] such women" (John 8:5, Lev. 20:10, Deut. 22:22–24). Jesus responded with something more profound and less archaic than a stiff literalism imposing the death penalty. He challenged "anyone . . . without sin" to throw the stones (John 8:7). After the crowd dispersed without throwing a single stone, Jesus forgave the woman instead of condemning her, while insisting that she change and not sin again (v. 11).

Third and perhaps most significantly, what was most important in his Bible? Without question, Jesus prioritized certain parts and de-emphasized others. For example, instead of understanding everything in the Bible as equally God's Word in a vacuum for anyone at any time, he focused his attention on the two greatest commandments: "You shall love the Lord your God with all your heart, and with all your soul, and with all your mind, and with all your strength," and "You shall love your neighbor as yourself" (Mark 12:30–31; Deut. 6:5, Lev. 19:18). Personally, I think these are intertwined. We daily live out our love of God by actively loving others.

Finally, Jesus did not restrict God's "voice" or prompting to action by putting a fence around every word, verse, or passage in his Bible. For example, he went beyond God's commandment of "You shall not murder" (Exod. 20:13; Deut. 5:17) to the heart of the injunction by speaking strongly against even being angry with or insulting another person (Matt. 5:22) and by blessing "the peacemakers . . . [as] children of God" (v. 9). Another example relates to God's command that "[y]ou shall not do any work" on the Sabbath (Exod. 20:10; Deut. 5:14). Some of Jesus's hard-line opponents severely criticized him for healing on the Sabbath (Mark 3:1–6). Jesus had a different and more humane view rooted in his consistent and supreme prioritization of loving others when he asked, "Is it lawful to do good or to do harm on the Sabbath, to save life or to kill?" (v. 4).

The Bible is a uniquely important collection of books for inquiry, study, and ethical direction. It is so important that it demands we use our *God-given* minds, attentiveness, inclination to question, and reflection so that we can better understand and authentically apply it toward qualitative living.

CHAPTER 5

A Rich, Humble, and Potentially Misunderstood Easter Model

T he numerous first Easter weekend accounts in the New Testament have some well-known participants, starting with Jesus appearing to many outside of his known tomb. Additionally, one or more angels comforted his frightened followers by telling them not to be afraid. Prominently, certain brave women ventured to his tomb on Easter Sunday out of respect to "anoint him" and complete customary burial rites (Mark 16:1).

According to the Gospel of Matthew's Good Friday account, "[m]any women," including those who risked approaching the tomb, "had followed Jesus from Galilee and had provided for him" (Matt. 27:55). What a powerful expression of Jesus's inclusiveness. In that archaic, male-centric time, Jesus had women followers and friends. Further, although Jesus focused most attention on the poor and other outcasts and encouraged his followers to prioritize their needs, he also had some rich acquaintances and apparent friends. A prominent example from the Gospel of John is Nicodemus, a Jewish leader who visited Rabbi Jesus at night with questions (John 3:1–16). Later, Nicodemus both opposed other leaders on behalf of Jesus (John 7:50–51) and participated in reverently following Jewish burial customs for Jesus after his death (John 19:39–40). Joseph of Arimathea partnered with Nicodemus, bravely going to Pilate to ask for his body so that these two rich and prominent men could respect and honor their friend Jesus in the traditional manner.

Let's focus attention on Joseph of Arimathea. All four New Testament Gospels include him in the Easter weekend accounts. Mark tells us he was "a respected member of the council, who was also himself waiting expectantly for the kingdom of God" (Mark 15:43). Matthew adds that he was a "rich man . . . who was also a disciple of Jesus" (Matt. 27:57). Luke notes that Joseph "was a good and righteous man . . . who, though a member of the council, had not agreed to their plan and action," that is, Jesus's death on the cross (Luke 23:50–51). Finally, John says Joseph "was a disciple of Jesus, though a secret one because of his fear of the Jews" (John 19:38). More accurately, Joseph's "fear" was of certain Jews in positions of immense power and influence because Joseph, Nicodemus, Jesus, and the initial followers of Jesus were all Jewish.

I think Joseph is mischaracterized in certain circles. I have heard some criticize and denounce Joseph for being a "secret" follower, as if he was ashamed or somehow fell short of being an actual early, Jewish Christian. I have a different perspective of Joseph, which is one of respect and as a potential role model. I see and understand Joseph as a profound example of an authentic follower and person of faith.

We read that all four New Testament Gospel writers knew about Joseph and spoke highly of him. Joseph was a disciple of Jesus and lived a good and righteous life. He bravely opposed the powerful council leaders who oppressed the poor and others whom Jesus routinely associated with and tried to help. He also courageously went to Pilate, the powerful Roman governor of Judea, risking his life to follow Jewish custom and honor Jesus in his death. The bottom line for me is that Joseph was both a fine Jewish and Christian person.

So, what do we do with the "secret" aspect of Joseph's discipleship? Perhaps we should understand that he sincerely endeavored during that time to live his faith as a Jewish man as well as following the teachings and example of Jesus the rabbi. He might also have been protecting his family, as well as his ability to potentially help Jesus as a member of the Jewish council during a crisis. Further, and this is something we can identify with today, maybe Joseph did not feel the need to always be name dropping "God" or "Jesus" like an advertisement to call attention to himself. Instead, he simply lived a good, active, and faith-observant life.

So, what can Joseph of Arimathea teach Christians (and anyone else) pursuing an ethically rewarding life during Easter or in any other season? As Paul says in his letter to the Colossians, God's chosen ones are those who live with "compassion, kindness, humility, gentleness, and patience," with love being the most important priority (Col. 3:12, 14).

CHAPTER 6

A Different View of Paradise Now—It's Our Choice

As I noted in an earlier chapter, I grew up in a conservative East Texas church. I heard a lot about "original sin" and "depravity" grounded in the garden of Eden account (Gen. 2:4–3:24) and the efficacy of Jesus dying on the cross to make things right. Most every week with minimal variation, the preacher "invited" us to walk the aisle and make a correct confession. Mere recitation of words made everything fine. A ticket to heaven—one and done—and avoidance of the fearful, eternal alternative. In *The Cost of Discipleship* (Macmillan 1959), Dietrich Bonhoeffer termed this "cheap grace," or mere assent to belief without a changed life in response to God's love. Fortunately, I had other influences in my childhood church who emphasized the ongoing priority to follow Jesus's example and teachings.

As a Christian, I certainly recognize the significance of the cross and of the resurrection of Jesus, which includes forgiveness (both God's of us and ours of others) and the opportunity for a new and changed life in God's kingdom, starting now. Over time, however, I altered my understanding of the creation accounts and the emphases of the first few chapters of the Bible. I also realize, like so much of Scripture, that there are different ways to understand the stories.

In context, Genesis (the first book of the Hebrew Bible/Old Testament) is an ancient book of (not "by") Moses. Chapters 1–11 contain archaic etiological stories (that is, stories of beginnings) from multiple sources, some with similarities to other ancient religious cultures. The accounts are ahistorical, meaning that despite the amount of time wasted arguing about the historicity of details, they are insignificant. Rather, like parables and mythology, the stories teach and point to more important truths.

One does not need to know Hebrew or take a religion course to immediately recognize that there are two creation stories in Genesis 1–3. Reading these chapters in any translation reveals a six-step-and-then-rest account followed by a very different, male-centric garden of Eden account.

As ancient as these stories are, they remain profoundly important. For me, combining parts of Genesis 1 with the story of Cain and Abel (in chapter 4) emphasizes equality, humanity's potential goodness, the importance of good choices, and the errors of tribalism. Further, linking these accounts plants important seeds for the Judeo-Christian emphasis on biblical "justice," namely, the importance of impartially loving and caring for the poor, ill, aliens (those from other cultures or countries), and other disadvantaged people. Indeed, seeking and working for justice is a priority in all authentic faith traditions and other roots of meaningful living.

The pinnacle of God's first creation account is us—humans: "So God created humankind in his image, in the image of God he created them, male and female he created them [and] God blessed them" (Gen. 1:27–28). After giving humans stewardship over all his creation, "God saw everything that he had made, and indeed, it was very good" (v. 31). So, we are created in God's image, which is far from depraved. Further, God creates us with equality (in gender and otherwise) and without reference to any divine preference of tribe, country, race, or any other differences.

When we transition to Genesis 4, we learn about Adam and Eve's first children, Cain (a farmer) and Abel (a shepherd) (vv. 1–2). Each made a religious offering to God, who "had regard for Abel and his offering" but not for "Cain and his offering." This made Cain "very angry" (vv. 3–5). Later, Cain invited Abel to join him in a field and "killed him" (v. 8). When God asked Cain for his brother's location, Cain lied and said, "I do not know; am I my brother's keeper?" (v. 9). The story in part demonstrates the evils of tribalism with historic hatred between "classes" of people, in this case farmers and shepherds.

Immediately before Cain murdered Abel, God said to Cain, "If you do well, will you not be accepted? And if you do not do well, sin is lurking at the door. Its desire is for you, but you must master it" (v. 7). This is the first biblical mention of "sin," which is wrongdoing. Essentially, sin is a bad choice of action. God's words signify to me two innate inclinations, one toward doing good and the other toward bad. We make day-to-day choices; good choices involve struggle and hard work. The heart of the story derives from Cain questioning God. Yes indeed, we *are* "keepers" and caretakers of other persons, irrespective of differences and group affiliations. As one another's keepers, we must make good daily choices rooted in love, care, and compassion.

So how do we understand the garden of Eden account? I'm not sure. Perhaps it is an ancient tale about acquiring knowledge of mortality, a sense of right and wrong, and the ability to make choices, as well as demonstrating enmity between (most) people and snakes.

In all seasons of our lives, each and every day, we should go out of our way to help others, particularly those less fortunate. From the beginning, we were created to make good choices rooted in love. Instead of a paradise lost for future restoration as some read the garden of Eden story, we can create *paradise now* by acting out of love for all, regardless of national, political, racial, and other divides.

CHAPTER 7

Does 1 + 1 + 1 Equal 2?

I am not an apocalyptic-oriented Christian for many reasons. Primarily, putting much time, hope, and energy into any miraculous future expectation is a distraction from focusing on practical daily discipleship. First generation Christians certainly expected Jesus to come again soon, perhaps to meet their messianic expectations of a powerful reign on earth and/or to trigger a resurrection of the dead and a rapture of living believers. Those with such expectations, even today, often refer to awaiting "the second coming."

In some of the apostle Paul's earliest New Testament letters, he emphasized the imminence of Jesus returning during his generation: "We will not all die, but we will be changed. . . . For the trumpet will sound, and the dead will be raised imperishable, and we will be changed" (1 Cor. 15:51–52). In 1 Thessalonians, probably the earliest New Testament book, Paul predicted that Jesus "will descend from heaven, and the dead in Christ will rise first. Then we who are alive . . . will be caught up in the clouds together with them . . . [to] be with the Lord forever" (1 Thess. 4:16–18). Yet, even in this context of imminent expectancy, Paul sternly warned against simply waiting around for it: "Anyone unwilling to work should not eat. For we hear that some of you are living in idleness, mere busybodies, not doing any work" (2 Thess. 3:10–11).

New Testament passages are not of one accord on this front. For example, in the Gospel of Mark (earliest of the four canonical gospels), Jesus summarizes his teaching and public ministry by saying, "The time is fulfilled, and the kingdom of God is at hand; repent, and believe in the good news" (Mark 1:14–15). Jesus appears to have said, "follow me" (e.g., Mark 1:17)—meaning follow his teachings and life-model as disciples—more than he asked anyone to wait. What was there to wait on, then or now, other than our own responsive living to Jesus's message and God's gift of one mortal life? As Jesus indicated when he started teaching, the kingdom is here, and it is high time to change the way we live.

In Mark 13, Jesus addressed the impending Roman destruction of the temple in Jerusalem, which occurred in 70 AD/CE, and his coming in "power and glory" (vv. 1–8, 26). Importantly, Jesus emphasized: "Truly I tell you, *this generation* will not pass away until all these things have taken place" (v. 30, emphasis added). We might also ask, what about one of the thieves crucified beside Jesus who asked Jesus to remember him in the afterdeath kingdom? Jesus responded: "Truly I tell you, today you will be with me in paradise" (Luke 23:43).

Jesus has already come twice: his birth and his resurrection, which Christians annually commemorate during Christmas and Easter, respectively. I have not extensively studied mathematics, but as I recall from elementary school, one plus one equals two.

Personally, I expect a heaven beyond this mortal life, fully united in and with God along with all who have crossed the river before and with others who cross later. Although I have no experience with it and am grateful to be alive, my expectation is akin to the thief on the cross, or, like a very quick light switch going off and then immediately back on. I expect the lights to go out at death and then quickly come on again as we go to God, transitioning to a brighter, eternal spiritual light and life. My hope is that within a nanosecond, we will shed this mortal body like a snakeskin (ashes to ashes, dust to dust) and that God will clothe us with an imperishable and eternal spiritual form.

The early Christians, hoping for yet another coming of Jesus according to parts of the New Testament, indicate their unrealized expectations of a messiah to deliver the Jews from Roman oppression. They yearn for a powerful, militaristic anointed one from God. Even Jesus's closest group of followers did not appear to fully "get it" during his lifetime. Instead of power, prestige, and miraculous events, God prioritizes (as he did in Judaism before Jesus) love, peace, and the pursuit of justice for the oppressed. Jesus prioritized these traits in the messianic kingdom, which he ushered in, encouraging his disciples (and us today) to follow his teachings and example by truly living out these characteristics in *this* life.

I do not think Jesus returning should be a divisive issue. "Another coming," while not my expectation, is essentially irrelevant. We as Christians, along with persons in other authentic faith traditions, and anyone else interested in meaningful living, should focus on what we are doing now—every single day. In the striking parable of the great judgment (Matt. 25:31–46), Jesus says, "God's blessing is on those who feed the hungry, provide water for the thirsty, welcome strangers, provide clothing for the needy, care for the sick, and visit prisoners" (vv. 34–40). These are all things *we can choose to actively do now*, living as agents of the kingdom in this life. Even Paul, with his common first-generation-Christian expectation of what would be a third coming, prioritizes the importance of how we live now, imploring his readers to live their lives "in a manner worthy of the gospel of Christ" (Phil. 1:27) and elsewhere insisting that "the only thing that counts is faith made effective through love" (Gal. 5:6).

Amidst disagreements and ambiguities about any expected future miraculous event, it is most certain that Jesus called people to follow his teachings and example of love and the pursuit of justice for the poor and others in need in this life, day-to-day. His emphasis is above and beyond any doctrinal disputes over future (as well as *current*) events. What are we doing now, whatever our stage of life? Let's not wait.

CHAPTER 8

The Pursuit of Justice: An Active Expression of Love and Inclusivity

I grew up during racially divisive and violent times in East Texas, especially due to the integration of Robert E. Lee High School during my sophomore year. Fear, rioting, and police patrols dominated most days. It was an unhappy time. I don't recall hearing about or experiencing much inclusion, love, nonviolence, or impartiality on our campus, much less in our community.

Biblical "justice" is among the most important scriptural and active pursuit priorities in Judeo-Christian tradition. Arguably, it is the number one faith priority for action as an expression of love in our world today. When I was in high school in the early 1970s, I did not think things could get much worse in terms of violence and hate-based racial divides. I realize now that I was wrong. Today's racial, political, economic, gender-based, and other forms of extremism seem even more outrageously polarized, intolerant, and violent—as if bombs are about to go off. Unfortunately, in too many cases, they do.

God's consistent insistence for persons to seek justice is prominent in the Hebrew Bible/Christian Old Testament and the New Testament. It covers countless generations with multiple sources over three thousand years or more, within many Biblical books and in a variety of contexts. Yet, do people of faith and others who similarly intend to live meaningfully really "get it"? For example, how far have we come (or regressed) in the United States since the Civil Rights Act of 1964, or as I note above, the violence I witnessed in high school in 1972–74?

Exercising justice means actively loving others who are vulnerable, disadvantaged, or otherwise in need. Justice is synonymous with "social justice" in contemporary terminology. However, I prefer the Biblical term: "justice." Adding "social" to anything in today's quick-to-judge-and-denigrate society is too politically charged. It seems to trigger some people who respond by rolling their eyes and tuning out, while others react even more negatively, immediately thinking of soundbites about socialism and lambasting the concept.

Seeking justice is *completely* apolitical, even though so many "politicize" it—as some folks tend to do with most anything they resist understanding. Exercising justice is neither liberal nor conservative nor anywhere in between. Rather, justice is love and inclusivity in action where it is needed most. It is easy to define but challenging to carry out. Justice is more important than worship, prayer, or any other religious custom or ritual. In fact, injustice in the alleged name of Christianity is a mockery, making expressions of faith hypocritical and meaningless.

Justice includes fair treatment and provision of opportunities for everyone in a society, with special emphasis and concern for the poor and any who are oppressed. This crucial emphasis on caring for others is always in season. Some cultural circumstances, however, cry out for prioritizing equity. An unfortunately recurring example is racially motivated murder or violence that breeds a violent aftermath. Injustice-induced violence predictably leads to violent protests. On both ends, the violence is misplaced. The peaceful resistance and strong advocacy for change embodied in the words and actions of Dr. Martin Luther King, Jr., is a model for a strong, unrelenting, and peaceful pursuit of justice.

A few Biblical examples from centuries-old sources highlight the central and timeless importance of justice, both for authentic people of faith and anyone else interested in a meaningful life.

Leviticus 19 is the ethical heart of the "Holiness Code" (Lev. 17–26). Through Moses, God told the people, "You shall be holy, for I the Lord your God am holy" (Lev. 19:2). This imperative goes all the way back to the first chapter of the Bible, which informs us that God created humankind in his image: "male and female he created them [and] God blessed them" (Gen. 1:27–28). As I emphasized previously, from the start, there were no tribes or favorites of any stripe. Rather, God made everyone in his own "image," which is both holy and wholly devoid of inherent depravity. Bad choices, such as violence and hatred between different groups, are the root of depravity. Leviticus 19 is the source of "you shall love your neighbor as yourself" (v. 18). Most people are familiar with this command, which Jesus also emphasized (Mark 12:31). A seldom referenced and often ignored later verse adds, "The alien [stranger] who resides with you shall be to you as the citizen among you. You shall love the alien as yourself" (Lev. 19:34). Jesus lived this and other aspects of justice out by associating with and attending to the poor and sick, tax collectors, and other social and religious outcasts of his time.

Many of the prophets, such as Isaiah and Amos, spoke strongly about justice to their own generations but with future applicability regarding similar contexts of injustice. Isaiah declared God's words: "[E]ven though you make many prayers, I will not listen; your hands are full of blood. Wash yourselves, make yourselves clean; remove the evil of your doings from before my eyes; cease to do evil, learn to do good; seek justice, rescue the oppressed, defend the orphan, plead for the widow . . . though your sins are like scarlet, they shall be as snow; though they are red like crimson, they shall become like wool. If you are willing and obedient, you shall eat the good of the land" (Isa. 1:15b–17, 18b–19). Thus, according to Isaiah, being "willing and obedient" to God's directive to seek justice appears to be a predicate of God's forgiveness.

Amos was another true champion of justice. In a passage called the "MLK, Jr. passage" by some because Dr. King utilized it, God spoke through Amos: "I hate, I despise your festivals, and I take no delight in your solemn assemblies. . . . Take away from me the noise of your songs; I will not listen to the melody of your harps. But let justice roll down like waters, and righteousness like an ever-flowing stream" (Amos 5:21, 23–24).

Justice is embedded in the fabric of Jewish-Christian tradition. In his embodiment and life-model of justice, Jesus drew on the very best of his Jewish tradition. So should we.

CHAPTER 9

Additional Focus on Jewish High Holy Days

I will not pretend to be an expert in Judaism or its important "high holy days," Rosh Hashanah (Jewish New Year) and Yom Kippur (Day of Atonement). Building to a certain extent on my emphasis in Chapter 2 on the important topic of Christians and Jewish holy days, I wholeheartedly believe that people who are not Jewish can learn and utilize so much from a mere elementary knowledge of these two high holy days and the encompassing time period. This includes persons in other faith traditions, as well as persons outside of any religious affiliation who aspire to live a life exhibiting high ethical and moral standards. As stated earlier in the book, I ask my Jewish friends and readers to understand if I mischaracterize or misunderstand any aspect or nuance of their important days, seasons, and traditions.

As a Christian, I am accustomed to learning from a Jewish rabbi who lived and taught two thousand years ago. Thus, I aspire to learn more about the religious contexts of Jesus's day to better understand his model and teachings. I also find it instructive to pay attention to and learn from Jewish friends and their customs and traditions today. This applies to other authentic faith traditions and practices as well. Unlike the frightening and violent racial and other extreme divisions on display in our country today, we should equitably and peacefully look for common ground, as well as paying attention to, respecting, and learning from different groups and ideas.

My understanding of Rosh Hashanah and Yom Kippur is that they form an important whole—*Yamim Noraim*—the Days of Awe. During this "season," Jews are encouraged to examine their deeds and misdeeds of the previous year. Through prayer and reflection, Jews are afforded the spiritual opportunity to do better in the coming year.

As a Christian, the annual period of Rosh Hashanah through Yom Kippur reminds me of what Lent and Easter can offer as a time for self-examination, recommitment, and forgiveness (of others and ourselves). I have always been puzzled by Christians historically paying so little, if any, attention to this important annual practice of our Jewish friends. As a Jewish rabbi in his time, Jesus would have taken part in such wonderful traditions.

My understanding is that Rosh Hashanah is rooted in portions of Leviticus in the Hebrew Bible/Christian Old Testament and focuses in part on thankfulness for God's creation. The culmination of the high holy days is Yom Kippur, which is based on reparations for wrongdoing and the requesting and giving of forgiveness so that we may get a "fresh start" in the new year.

Of great interest to me is the deeply personal experience of this time. This intentional and intense ten-day period of personal faith and of the life-related examination of one's past year illustrates the underlying theology of Judaism: that each of us is given the opportunity to transform and renew through atonement. Stated differently, this annual hard and honest look at how one has lived relative to one's priorities in faith and in life over the past year should lead to repentance toward authentic, actual changes in day-to-day living.

During this time, many congregants gather near water and utilize comforting words from the prophet Micah, including, "[God] will again have compassion upon us; he will tread our iniquities under foot. [God] will cast all our sins into the depths of the sea" (Mic. 7:19). What a vivid ritual and image for letting go of every low part of the prior year to start anew.

Rabbi Harold Kushner expresses the potential experience and result of these high holy days in his characteristically wise and practical manner. In a chapter dynamically titled "The Future Can Change the Past" in his recent book, *Echoes of Sinai* (Curtis Brown Studios 2018), he vividly describes how transformative the experience can be when observed with absolute seriousness. (I utilized this same chapter above in Part II, Chapter 2). Per Rabbi Kushner, "It can liberate you from your shadow . . . and let your new self emerge [with] a brand-new start. . . . [R]ather than the person you have too often settled for being [y]ou will have become the person God has wanted you to be all along."

Christians (or anyone else) adopting a similar framework at any time of the year can enhance our respective faith journeys and ethical quality of life. The model includes important steps:

1. Intentional annual self-examination;
2. Accepting God's and our own forgiveness;
3. Asking forgiveness of people we might have wronged in some way;
4. Resolving with God's help to transform who we are and how we act;
5. Engaging in the hard, disciplined work to make it happen.

For Christians, using Lent (culminating in the celebration of new life at Easter) might be an ideal framework. We could look at the time period as an annual reawakening to truly repent and change, as well as celebrating what we believe happened long ago.

There is no magic in the time or frequency with which we follow these or similar steps, only in the seriousness and regularity of the spiritual practices. We can go through similar periods of introspection whenever we need them to effectuate positive changes in living, including loving and respecting others and treating all with equity.

CHAPTER 10

How a Systematic Approach Enhances Consistent Qualitative Living

I f you play golf, then you know the frustration between very good and very bad rounds. This is true of many other games and habits that are supposed to be fun! Just when you think you "get it" and have found the secret to improvement during a great day of golf, you return the next day to an abominable performance. If you don't play or like golf, please bear with me a minute as I transition from golf to the variation in the quality of our day-to-day lives.

If you live in or anywhere near Austin, Texas—or if you live anywhere and play golf—then you have probably heard of Harvey Penick. Mr. Penick is best known for his character, which included kindness, gentleness, and empathy. He was a devoted friend to so many people. He was also one of the best golf teachers who ever lived, utilizing simple, non-technical, time-proven wisdom and suggestions. He wrote the best-selling *Harvey Penick's Little Red Book* (Simon & Schuster 1992). His "Red Book" was so popular that he followed it with his "Green Book," titled *And If You Play Golf, You're My Friend* (Simon & Schuster 1993). His wisdom and perspective go beyond golf and golfers and apply to everyone. Penick's influential writing centered on consistent moral living, focused on helping others.

In a chapter in the Green Book titled "The Erratics," Mr. Penick has a very practical suggestion for golfers who can't string together consistently good scores. He suggests golfers keep a meticulous diary connected to wildly erratic rounds (e.g., what they ate, how they slept, who were they with, and the like). These accounts provide personal hints toward a greater percentage of good outings.

Enough about golf. My intent was to set the stage for how Mr. Penick's wisdom profoundly keys into greater consistency in daily qualitative living, such as actually living the most important aspects of authentic faith traditions, including love, peacefulness, gentleness, and caring for the needy. I think most of us through our experiences recognize the vast and variable spectrum of successfully implementing these fine qualities day to day.

Is this extensive variance in our degree of high-quality living purely arbitrary and unpredictable? Do we just unexpectedly have morally deficient, throw-it-away type days and conclude, "Oh well, it was just a bad day. I'll see what tomorrow brings"?

No one is perfect. We all have bad days. Nevertheless, we *do* have the potential to consistently control good and effective days where we focus on and intentionally live in line with our moral and authentically faith-based priorities. What is a key ingredient? *Daily preparation.*

The earliest New Testament Gospel, Mark, implies that Jesus had an early morning routine of prayerful solitude before actively beginning his day: "In the morning, while it was still very dark, he got up and went out to a deserted place, and there he prayed" (Mark 1:35). The author tells us in the next few verses that Jesus's followers "hunted" him down, and then they were ready to go to work.

Observing an intentional, first-part-of-the-day practice helps to steer us in the correct direction. Otherwise, our number of truly good days, ones where we are fully present and actively caring, humble, respectful, compassionate, and loving, will suffer. How we set our mind right as the day begins is a matter of personal preference, with flexibility to alter our routine when results indicate its ineffectiveness.

People who knew Harvey Penick loved him dearly because he consistently exercised kindness, humility, and gentleness toward everyone. Golf was simply his context for helping people and developing numerous meaningful friendships. He was a magnetic role model for behavior. I think being outside in nature each day and making people happier by enhancing their enjoyment of a shared hobby combined into a type of "routine" for consistently living a meaningful daily life. Mr. Penick certainly left a strong mark in this world with everyone he met, which is an important aspect of our immortality.

As mentioned earlier, Mr. Penick's chapter "The Erratics" addresses the extremes of performance. One way we can apply his counsel to the significance of our daily living is by doing what he suggests, which is asking ourselves, "Was my mind clear and my heart serene?" That is a powerful inquiry for reflecting on each day as it ends, and for resolving to awake to a fresh opportunity tomorrow.

Toward the end of his Green Book, Mr. Penick includes a short entry titled "My Prayer." His prayer ends with a deep, selfless, and profound petition: "Guide us and direct us in your way of life, that this will be a better world because we have lived in it."

CHAPTER 11

We Should Care About Everyone

As a child, when I was frustrated about something or in a bad mood, I would often reply to my parents' questions with, "I don't care." Invariably, my mother would respond, "Honey, let's not say that. You should care about everything and everyone." As an adult, when I slip toward my "not caring" mode, I hear my mom's words as if she was in the room with me. Indeed, she is with me—at a minimum through the lasting imprint of her life-model and words of wisdom.

When I was a child, polio was eradicated with a vaccine. Wouldn't it be great if we developed a fully effective vaccine to eliminate hatred and discrimination and replace them with understanding, compassion, and love for everyone? Unfortunately, there is no immediate "cure" to bring our factious country and world together. Nevertheless, we can choose to make this transition. Unlike a momentary shot in the arm with a dose of vaccine, this type of change requires intention, hard work, and time. Without question, the time is now for us to start. Truly caring about making—and actively living—such a repentance from guarded tribalism toward respect, tolerance, and inclusiveness is our first step.

What does it mean to truly "care" about other people who differ from us in any way? Caring is multifaceted. At its heart, we can begin to dissolve judgment and prejudice, coming together peacefully by: (1) actually and empathetically listening to others, and (2) finding and emphasizing common ground instead of accentuating differences.

Listening is an art, and sometimes, a lost one. Listening to others takes effort, resolve, and practice when we aspire to transform it into a habit. The author of the New Testament book of James instructs his readers, "You must understand this, my beloved: let everyone be quick to listen, slow to speak, slow to anger" (James 1:19). The apocryphal book of Sirach (part of the Catholic Bible but not the Hebrew Bible or Protestant Old Testament) is full of wise sayings related to the importance of listening. Examples include: (1) "Be quick to hear but deliberate in answering" (Sir. 5:11); (2) "If you love to listen you will gain knowledge, and if you pay attention you will become wise" (6:33), and (3) "Before you speak, learn" (18:19a).

In essence, listening involves learning about and appreciating another's perspective, respectfully not interrupting, paying mindful and open attention to what someone else says, and then pausing and deliberately breathing to relax before you respond. In sum, listening is part of peaceful and constructive dialogue and other communication toward tolerance and understanding.

Our goal in faith-related and other dialogue with persons from different traditions and walks of life should *not* be to "save" them by convincing them to consent that our way of believing or seeing things is correct. Rather, our objectives should include understanding, respect, humility, and learning.

In addition to talking with one another and prioritizing authentic listening, we should endeavor to find commonalities with others. In fact, this should be a primary goal of respectful dialogue. Regarding interfaith and intra-faith differences of opinion, as well as disparities of political and other perspectives between people regardless of faith affiliation, we can create—as well as find—action based common ground. How about simply doing good for others, such as working together to help the sick, hungry, poor, oppressed, and others who are suffering or in need? This can be a starting and ending point and a key to mutual "salvation" devoid of advocacy of opinion.

Practically, what might our common efforts look like? The possibilities and opportunities are seemingly endless. Some examples include joining together and serving a meal to the hungry, collecting blankets and warm clothes for winter months, writing friendly letters as pen pals to lonely prisoners, mentoring and being positive role models to children who need help, and adopting rescue dogs or cats (love of animals creates strong bonds).

With the multiplicity of needs around us all, acting together to practically care about and for others has a healing effect on group-based and other fractured relationships. Differences in belief or opinion can take a back seat to other priorities. Further, it might transform the nature of further dialogue with one another, making it easier to live together with tolerance and respect by working together to do good.

CHAPTER 12

Learning From Experience: The Universal Teacher

"Religious experience is inevitably human experience." Thich Nhat Hanh, an inclusive Buddhist writer, penned these wise, real-life centric words in his compelling book, *Living Buddha, Living Christ* (Riverhead Books 1995). Hanh draws insightful and compelling parallels between Buddhism and Christianity. His thoughts are rooted in his diverse experiences, meditation, and consistent daily practice of mindfully paying attention. Hanh's perspective and suggestions are helpful to anyone seeking a grounded, compassionate, and peaceful life, whether faith-based or otherwise. His calm, peaceful, and wise manners emanate through his pen in everything he writes.

Although people often treat them separately, religion and daily life are not distinct parts of life. Rather, they should form an intertwined whole. From a faith-based perspective, worship, tradition, liturgical seasons, sacred texts, study, prayer, and meditation are examples of our religious dimensions and experiences. However, there is more to our faith-based lives than such traditional aspects.

Learning from life experiences is arguably one of the most underrated components of any authentic faith tradition, as well as simply pursuing a meaningful life apart from any such tradition. "Life experiences" include parts of our own lives, observations of others, and what we learn from respected mentors and teachers. From a biblical studies perspective, we often collectively term the whole of this as "wisdom."

How do we learn from life experiences? We must pay close and consistent attention to them, periodically and intentionally reflect upon them, and then determine and implement changes to improve our life qualitatively. In our reflection on how we have lived, we can carefully consider our thoughts—and especially our actions—toward others and ourselves, along with how others have treated us. What is helpful and harmful to us? What key parts of our lives do we need to alter? Inevitably, we should be drawn to compassionate, empathetic, inclusive, kind, and caring lifestyles. In a nutshell, we should be "love-centric" in all that we do and speak. Although the concept is basic and might sound simplistic, truly practicing it requires hard, disciplined work.

In my Judeo-Christian tradition, we identify certain books of the Bible as "wisdom literature." One of the best-known books in this genre is Proverbs. From its inception, Proverbs highlights "learning about wisdom and instruction" and "gaining instruction in wise dealing, righteousness, justice, and equity" (Prov. 1:2–3). The writer's personification of Wisdom notes that God created Wisdom "at the beginning of his work . . . before the beginning of the earth" (Prov. 8:22–23). Further, Wisdom "was beside [God] like a master worker . . . rejoicing in his inhabited world and delighting in the human race" (Prov. 8:30–31).

The Gospel of John begins with a prologue that is among the most developed New Testament deification passages. Among other things, John's signposting starts by announcing, "In the beginning was the Word [which Christians identify as Jesus], and the Word was with God, and the Word was God" (John 1:1). Further, everything "came into being through him"; "in him was life [and] the life was the light of all people"; "the Word became flesh and lived among us" (John 1:3-4 and 14).

John was the last-written of the Gospels. It starts out very different from Mark, the earliest Gospel. In contrast to John, Mark notes at the outset that the "beginning of the good news of Jesus Christ" was at the time of "John the baptizer," including John's baptism of an adult Jesus and the start of Jesus's ministry as a Jewish rabbi (Mark 1:1, 4, 9, 14–15).

Regarding John's lofty assertions, Christians often focus interpretive attention on the Greek term for "Word," which is *logos*, meaning "speech" or "reason." In contrast, I think "Word" keys into Christianity's Jewish roots and the concept of Wisdom. The apocryphal books (included in Catholic but not Protestant Scripture) of Sirach and the Wisdom of Solomon offer significant parallels. Both books were written within two hundred years of Jesus's birth and augment Proverbs in describing Wisdom. For example, Wisdom "is a breath of the power of God, and a pure emanation of [God]. . . . She is a reflection of eternal light . . . and an image of his goodness. . . . She renews all things . . . [and] God loves nothing so much as the person who lives with wisdom" (Wisd. of Sol. 7:25–28). Further, Wisdom "came forth from the mouth of [God]. . . . Before the ages, in the beginning, [God] created me, and for all the ages, I shall not cease to be" (Sir. 24:3, 9).

True wisdom that results in meaningful living derives from thoughtful reflection upon and actively learning from tangible, day-to-day experiences. We all have personal experiences and the opportunity to observes others' lives. Thus, the power of wisdom is potentially available to everyone, provided we pay attention and apply what we can learn. As Hanh advises regarding life experience, reflection, and the meaningful practice of life, "Looking deeply at our own mind and our own life, we will begin to see what to do and what not to do to bring about a real change. . . . Our faith must be alive. It cannot be just a set of rigid beliefs and notions. . . . Faith implies practice, living our daily life in mindfulness."

CHAPTER 13

One Thematic Word for Daily Emphasis and Living

One word is not much, but it can infuse a day with meaningfulness beyond words. A simple routine of choosing a stellar and aspirational characteristic can make the ordinary extraordinary. In fact, such a practice can make what we think of as "just another day," which many might think is boring, the most important thing in our lives.

I am a routine-oriented person. I think a daily preparatory practice enhances our potential for a well-lived, intentional, and focused day. Daily meditative time is a matter of personal choice and varies in numerous ways, including by time of day, duration, content, and place. For most daily practitioners, solitude, stillness, and quiet are fundamentals. However, "stillness" does not always mean sitting or otherwise staying in the same place. Some people experience meditative mental stillness in movement, especially by walking in a natural setting, such as beside a still body of water. Whatever the particulars, a personal, focused daily time for reflection and quiet is a wonderful enablement vehicle toward high-quality ethical meaning, both for us and for the others we encounter during each day.

In my view, authentic religious traditions not only involve simply striving to be a good person, but also share common characteristic traits for our lives. In my Christian tradition, a special passage in Paul's letter to the Colossians includes a representative list of what I consider important traits to implement in the practice of life. By "practice," I mean actual living as opposed to athletic, musical, or other contexts of preparing for a game or event. Life is not an upcoming game or stage performance. Rather, it is our real, tangible, daily activities and related intentions: everything we think, say, and do. Just like "practicing" medicine, law, or another profession or skill, we hope our art of living progresses each day in quality and meaningfulness. Daily routines, including characteristic focal points, can truly help us accomplish this.

In Colossians 3:12–16, Paul lists several characteristics as examples of practical focal points: (1) compassion, (2) kindness, (3) humility, (4) gentleness, (5) patience, (6) peace, and (7) gratitude. As a starting point, these seven attributes could be our key thoughts to put into action over a week's time. These characteristics have one key thing in common: They are active intentions and expressions of love. As Paul says within this passage, "Above all, clothe yourselves with love, which binds everything together in perfect harmony" (Col. 3:14).

As an example, think about *compassion* as our one-word "mission statement" for a day. What might that look like in practice? With a mindful, moment-by-moment implementation, such consistent focus during our waking hours could transform everything we do, including how we treat others and how we approach our work. If we start at home, with compassion as our motivation when interacting with our families, we might well be more sensitive to our family members' needs and empathetic toward their feelings. At our workplace, we would tend to be more helpful, less selfish, and better listeners. If we work hard at being compassionate in a commercially oriented work setting, some people we work with might even think, "Who is this person?"

When encountering strangers in obvious need, a focus on compassion might translate into sensitivity and generosity. With all people we encounter (including other drivers on busy roads) during our compassion-filled day, we might try being friendlier than usual and smiling more. At the end of the day, we could potentially be filled with a sense of happiness, which transcends the day, as opposed to a sense of frustration or discontentment toward the day.

What about how we treat ourselves? With compassion as our priority, we might just give ourselves a break from habitual nit-picking, judgment, and rushing through a multitude of things we think we "must" accomplish. We might collectively find that in most aspects of our day, we slowed down and actually paid attention to the people and activities around us, including our own peace of mind.

Choosing a desirable daily trait—perhaps one we might already admire in other people in our lives; one that makes us feel loved and like the center of their attention—is a simple concept, yet it is challenging to successfully implement and focus on staying on point. With regular practice, however, we can improve and build upon our choice and implementation of fine personal qualities by living one day at a time.

CHAPTER 14

God's Plan Is the Same for Everyone

"God has a particular plan for your life." I heard that over and over in church settings growing up. Wow, that seemed like such a unique and special thing! Trying to uncover it, however, was like the proverbial search for a needle in a haystack. The well-intentioned meaning of these unsolicited "prophets" for my life caused me varying degrees of trauma, as well as downright guilt during adolescence and into my early college years. I sensed an unnecessary pressure. I struggled mightily both to discover and implement the alleged "secretive plan" so that I could walk through the door to my faith-related life, which always seemed to relate to some vocational "calling."

In retrospect, I perceive things so very differently now. While I respect other people who think in such terms, I see a few potential flaws with this idea. First, it is overly self-focused. Narcissistic is too strong of a word, but constantly looking in a mirror to figure out God's so-called unique purpose for one's life is an insular endeavor that can prevent us from seeing others who need us.

More significantly, I strongly believe God's "plan" for everyone is identical. In a nutshell: We are to love others impartially. As a Christian, Jesus's life-model and teachings present a roadmap for the "narrow . . . way [that] is hard [and] that leads to life, and . . . few . . . find it" (Matt. 7:14). In line with Jesus's Jewish tradition, we walk properly—living step by step—when we are "holy" because "God [is] holy" (Lev. 19:2).

What does holiness look like? Practically, God intends, and indeed commands, us to be holy by loving, in a practical sense, our "neighbor" as well as "the alien," meaning anyone who is different (Lev. 19:18, 34). Quoting Leviticus, Jesus similarly prioritized loving others (Mark 12:31). The author of the New Testament epistle of 1 John tells us that "God is love" and that "everyone who loves is born of God and knows God" (1 John 4:16, 7).

Whether Christian, Jewish, a follower of another authentic faith tradition, or simply someone endeavoring to be a good person, we all have the same vocation. Our common calling is to love each other. As noted in the previous chapter, the apostle Paul adds other superlative qualities that are all under the sacred umbrella of love: "compassion, kindness, humility, gentleness, and patience" (Col. 3:12), as well as "joy, peace . . . generosity . . . and self-control" (Gal. 5:22–23). Drawing again from the prior chapter, if we simply pick one or a few of these character traits and work hard to truly live them each day, then we will be living in a loving manner.

Some things that often pass for "religion" in word and deed these days are inconsistent with these love-oriented characteristics. For example, any actions or words rooted in hatred, exclusivity, violence, arrogance, or partiality miss the mark and reek of inauthenticity if not downright hypocrisy. As a Christian, I do not associate any such characteristics with Jesus. As a religious person more generally, I also reject them as irreligious. Finally, simply as a human being, I reject them as inhumane and indecent.

Although we all have the same love-based priority for meaningful living, we are still unique individuals. In contrast to digging for some pre-determined "plan" to discover like a personalized but buried key, we can instead introspectively and intentionally reflect upon our gifts, talents, circumstances, and opportunities. This means looking into our hearts, minds, and experiences rather than constantly into a mirror. We peer into ourselves so that we can make wise, self-determined, and good choices during our respective gifts of one mortal life. How will we spend our time and talents? How can we most effectively love, care for, and help others in our life circumstances? Our circumstances are certainly not static, so we should periodically rethink how we are living and what changes might be in order.

When my wife and I first married, we lived in what for us at the time was a nice apartment. The bay window was my favorite spot. On a sunny day, we could look out this window and see blue sky and many different people, all God's children. There was no reflection; we could only look out and see others. I think that is God's chosen perspective for all people—to look upon others in their diverse life settings and really see and embrace them, considering if we can help them in any way. Whoever you are, can you imagine a higher calling?

CHAPTER 15

Character

My paternal grandfather, whom we called Granddad-dy, was a real character with a big-kid persona. He had a great sense of humor and was always fun to be around. He was a mountain of a man physically, with a gentle nature and a huge heart. What a great combination for a grand-father to a kid like me. I was so very fortunate to have him in my life. I dearly loved my grandmother as well, including her homemade cooking and her devotion to all in our family.

My grandparents modeled a healthy relationship in many ways. Yet, my grandmother's elevated frustration threshold had its limits, especially related to communication. Granddaddy wore hearing aids, yet he seemed to selectively hear what he liked, such as his favorite television show, *Gunsmoke*. I vividly recall numerous instances at the dinner table when my grandmother would begin asking him questions and reeling off chores for him as he quietly ate with his head down. Her voice rising, she would often get up, walk to his side, and scream, "Russell" in his ear. This was followed by a loud, responsive, "What?" As kids, when we were not in trouble, we deviously anticipated these scenes.

As a young teenager, I worked for my grandfather at his used car lot. In addition to the fun of just being around him, trips to their home for nap-inducing lunches, and daily mid-afternoon walks across the street for pie and coffee breaks, I learned something of lasting and profound importance. I closely watched Granddaddy carry out his business with personal relationships and a respectful manner toward everyone he encountered. In the context of the late 1960s and early 1970s in East Texas, with a hateful and discriminatory perspective lurking all around, he treated everyone the same. I vividly recall him, tobacco in his mouth and spittoon close by, sitting in his office and dealing with a diverse clientele one person at a time. He was kind, understanding, fair, and gentle in his demeanor and communication with everyone—black, white, Hispanic, male, female, or any anyone else.

What really stands out in retrospect is my grandfather's compassion, which is simply a word to characterize love-based, meaningful action. Most of his diverse customers had one thing in common: They were hard-working people who needed transportation to work so that they could get by and care for their families. Many of them could not afford to pay cash on the spot or obtain financing for a car.

I recall Granddaddy often asking what a person who was in dire need of a car could pay on a weekly basis. This approach led to his weekly Saturday morning practice of opening his office for the sole purpose of customers making weekly payments without interest, usually in cash because most of them had no bank account. He kept envelopes full of cash with names on one side and a handwritten ledger of sorts, noting dates and payments until paid in full.

My parents, aunt, and uncle worried so much about him as he continued his work until his untimely death at age seventy-five. He was an aging, nice, and trusting man alone in that office with a large amount of cash that his numerous repeat customers all knew about. Each one could see the pile of money a few feet away as he opened his drawer for them to pay what they could afford. Yet, I never heard about any hint of a problem with anyone.

I was there a few times with him on Saturdays, washing or wiping down cars but primarily just sitting outside his office in the very small reception area. I remember that he smiled, knew people's names, asked about their families and the cars they bought, showed them their accounts, and wished them a good week ahead—one at a time. From the customers, I recall firm handshakes, return smiles, thank-yous, and, "See you next week." Although I woke up and went to church the next morning, I had already been to "real" church Saturday morning by observing these kind, honest, respectful, inclusive, and peaceful human interactions. That is what true Christianity, any other active faith, or simply a decent life is all about.

From the standpoint of hate-, violence-, and judgment-laced racial, economic, and religious prejudice, things are not much different in our country now than they were fifty-plus years ago in East Texas and many other places in our country. "Systemic" racism and other forms of discrimination are prominent in our time. I am no expert, but to me the terminology signifies historic, continuing, and potentially contemporary worsening of deeply pervasive and ingrained oppression.

What can we do individually about such an overwhelming cultural pandemic for which there is no short-term permanent fix? The answer is *something*. The something starts with compassionate and equal treatment of everyone individually. Imagine the cumulative effect of such one-on-one action by a multitude of well-intentioned people? As Bishop Michael Curry describes in his practical and memoir-like book, *Love Is the Way* (Penguin Random House 2020), we can focus on "one relationship at a time" to work for change. If we start now, person-to-person and one step at a time with continuity, effective progress will be our result—and much-needed reward. We should all take these steps every day.

CHAPTER 16

What Truly Matters?

Decades ago, in my first election as an eligible voter, I recall a strange conversation with an acquaintance. He was a bit more conservative in his Christian outlook and initiated the conversation by asking about my voting choices, which is not necessarily a good icebreaker for friendly conversation. I took the bait and told him. His response? "Oh no, he's just a 'do-gooder.' Instead, you should vote for a 'Christian.'" He explained to me in a dictatorial manner that his idea of a "Christian" candidate was simply a litmus test based on one or two social and personal issues, which he judged as measures of godliness (or not). I kept my mouth shut and came up with a reason for a quick departure because a mutually respectful conversation in that moment seemed unlikely.

Setting politics completely aside, I recall the disdain with which my young acquaintance mockingly pronounced "do-gooder." My head-shaking reaction now, as it was then, is total bewilderment. Anyone who does good for others in the way they live daily is a mentor and role model, not someone subject to mockery because they hold varying opinions on certain politically charged issues.

Recently, I have read and heard berating descriptions of "liberal Christians" who, instead of insisting on the prominence of believing factually in miracles and the bodily resurrection of Jesus, focus upon and highlight Jesus as a teacher who prioritized love, inclusiveness, and the pursuit of justice. Personally, I choose to believe in both miracles and Jesus's resurrection. However, following the teachings and life-model of Jesus is both the most prominent and important aspect of being Christian and intersects with the core of other authentic faith traditions, as well as simply being a model human being.

As a Christian, it is an easy step to emphasize what Jesus taught and modeled as of first importance while still understanding that this priority does not eliminate what one chooses to believe happened historically or miraculously. The New Testament Gospels repeatedly depict Jesus saying, "Follow me" during his public ministry (e.g., Mark 1:16–20). In fact, John 21 reports a post-resurrection appearance of Jesus to some of his disciples in which he cooked breakfast for them (ever the model of service to others) and then again emphasized the necessity of "following" him (John 21:19).

"Belief police" who judgmentally insist on "correct" historical or current beliefs as necessities for being accepted by God and going to heaven often utilize snippets from the apostle Paul's letters. For example, I grew up hearing Ephesians 2:8–9 repeatedly cited in a context-void vacuum, a "this is all that matters" creedal manner: "For by grace you have been saved through faith, and this is not your own doing; it is the gift of God— not the result of works, so that no one may boast." Yet, how about adding the very next verse? "For we are what he has made us, created in Christ Jesus for good works, which God prepared beforehand to be our way of life" (Eph. 2:10). Thus, *God made us to be "do-gooders!"*

Further in Ephesians, Paul emphatically pleads with his readers: "[I] beg you to lead a life worthy of the calling to which you have been called, with all humility and gentleness, with patience, bearing with one another in love, making every effort to maintain the unity of the Spirit in the bond of peace" (Eph. 4:1–3).

Paul pleaded with his readers to live consistently by following Jesus because he understood it as the number one priority for early Christians. The same has applied to generations since and should be our priority today.

Reading and prayerfully thinking about the entirety of Paul's first-century correspondence strongly indicates that he understood that how followers of Jesus lived was critically important *along with* their beliefs. In his culture, "belief" and "following" by living a changed life based on Jesus's teachings were intertwined. In contrast, in our contemporary American culture, "belief" can often have a non-substantive, surficial sense of merely assenting to certain "truths" without any noticeable impact on a person's daily life. That is simply inauthentic belief.

We live in an era of polarization, tribalism, and demonization. Hateful categorization of people who are different or think differently as "liberal" or "conservative" (or worse characterizations) are symptomatic of our diseased time. We would all be better off taking steps toward cultural transformation by finding common ground with others, starting with working together to do good things for others instead of insisting on allegedly correct or incorrect doctrines or opinions that drive larger wedges between us.

CHAPTER 17

Jesus Is Synonymous with Social Justice[1]

Without qualification, truly following Jesus means prioritizing the active pursuit of justice every day of our lives. The imperative root of this emphasis is at the heart of Judaism as understood by Jesus. From greeting and treating all people, especially those who differ from us, in an equally friendly and impartial manner, to supporting policies and requirements for fair and ethical treatment of currently or formerly disadvantaged or oppressed persons, it is high time for justice without delay. Fundamentally, this is love expressed in practical daily living. Time is of the essence for change—there is a sense of profound urgency for strong, active, and effective pursuit of justice.

For Christians, advocating justice in word and more particularly deed is a mandate because being Christian means to live according to the life-model and teachings of Jesus. As I have noted many times in this book, Jesus said countless times in the New Testament Gospels, to people of his time and to us today, "Follow

---

1. The Mindful Word originally posted a variant of this article at www.the-mindfulword.org/2021/jesus-cultural-transformation/

me." For non-Christians who hold to other faith traditions or who simply aspire to live in a meaningfully and impactful manner, Jesus offers a stellar example as well.

Unfortunately, what often passes for "Christian" in the public and political square of our American culture does not remotely reflect what Jesus taught and lived. In fact, the public face of Christianity often reeks of exclusivity, violence, and the pursuit of power, which makes it unrecognizable as connected in any way with Jesus.

Parts of Luke 3 and 4, when considered alongside Jesus's lifetime of helping and actively caring for the sick, outcasts, oppressed, poor, and other disadvantaged persons, highlight the primacy of the pursuit of justice. The authentic truth is that Jesus experienced something vocationally formative at his baptism (Luke 3:21–22). Subsequently, he retreated in solitude to the deserted wilderness to struggle with his calling (Luke 4:1–13) and how he should react to his special sensory baptismal light.

In Judeo-Christian terminology, this introspective and formative time in solitude related to what type of messiah or "anointed one" he would be, model, and teach during his life. He struggled mightily, as personified by the "devil" tempting him in wrong directions, as many people, including some of his followers, more than likely did up until his death. As the author of Luke describes, Jesus said "no" to temptations toward extreme worldly power (e.g., military or political) or becoming an overtly miraculous showman (Luke 4:5–12) as he dug deeply for his correct path.

So, what resulted from Jesus's extensive baptismal and messianic audit in the wilderness? Clarity! Luke describes Jesus emerging from his solitary grappling with doubt with a definitive understanding of his mission, which should also be the mission of all Christians and other persons of goodwill who want to live in a truly love-based manner. Jesus came forth full of the "power of the Spirit" (Luke 4:14), essentially meaning with God's direction, companionship, and partnership. Jesus went to the synagogue in Nazareth (v. 16), where, drawing from Isaiah (one of several prophetic champions of justice in his Jewish tradition), he announced at the outset of and as a signpost to the entirety of his public ministry, "The Spirit of the Lord is upon me, because he has anointed me to bring good news to the poor. He has sent me to proclaim release to the captives and recovery of sight to the blind, to let the oppressed go free, to proclaim the year of the Lord's favor" (vv. 18-19).

Having rejected power and overt miracle-working (i.e., putting on a show for all to see), Jesus embraced the cause of the poor and oppressed as his own. That indeed is what we should do as his followers and as people who are fed up with the extremes of judgment, inequality, partiality, violence, and oppression.

In his letter to the Ephesians a few decades after the life and teachings of Jesus (which was probably more of a circular letter to several churches in Asia Minor), St. Paul aptly stated, "Be careful then how you live, not as unwise people but as wise, making the most of the time, because the days are evil" (Eph. 5:15–16).

As of this writing, we are almost sixty years past the enactment of the Civil Rights Act in 1964. Arguably, things are no better, and potentially worse, than in the 1960s, in both subtle and overt ways. We are in trouble in America. Our days are certainly "evil" in regard to how certain people and groups are consistently treated. We need to be very "careful" and intentional in how we live and respond to inequity because our mortal lives are limited. It is high time, right now and without any further delay, for a full-scale cultural transformation not only in the name of Christianity and the ways of Jesus but also in the spirit of humanity and decency.

CHAPTER 18

Tribalism Was the Real "Fall" of Mankind: It Is High Time for Us to Get Up

What has always "tainted" mankind from ethical, inclusive, and caring living, and is still the root of our contemporary cultural divide? Bad choices, including ones often rooted in tribe-based anger and hatred.

This chapter revisits some of the emphases in Chapter 6 related to the two creation stories in Genesis 1–3 and the account of Cain and Abel in Genesis 4. These formative and insightful accounts deserve that we revisit them, bringing attention to both their similarities and a few different twists in our examination.

Generally, the first four chapters of the Bible, Genesis 1–4, contain parable-like ancient stories that contain profound truths. They are best considered ahistorical etiological accounts, which means mythlike stories of beginnings. How did it all begin and then start to go wrong? These archaic stories contain insightful truths and wisdom.

Genesis 1–3 includes what many consider two creation accounts from separate sources: first, one of six steps/days and then rest (chapter 1), followed by the all-too-well-known garden of Eden and banishment in chapters 2 and 3. I grew up with way too much emphasis on the literal garden of Eden account and the so-called "fall of mankind." Although there is more to the story and many ascribe significant importance to various aspects of the account, in a nutshell, this quasi-traditional approach makes Adam and Eve disobeying an arbitrary rule about avoiding certain fruit on the advice of a snake result in the "need" for Jesus to make things right on the cross.

As a Christian, I believe that Jesus does make things right by showing and teaching us how to live. Further, I personally and strongly believe that his death and resurrection can result in forgiveness, profound peace, and companionship, and that they enable us to make good choices. That is what true, light-filled life in the kingdom of God is all about now—good choices. Jesus's teachings and model of living provide the foundations for an inclusive, love-centered life for Christians and everyone else.

The well-known six-step or "day" creation account culminates in God's creation of humankind: "God created humankind in his image, in the image of God he created them, male and female he created them" (Gen. 1:27). Further, "God saw everything that he had made, and indeed, it was very good" (Gen. 1:31). Thus, the climactic lasting truth of this account is that from the very start, humans were both very good and equal to each other. The only distinction was gender. The story does not even hint at groups, races, economic gaps, or any tribal or other differences.

Temporarily setting aside the separate garden of Eden account in Genesis 2 and 3, linking the complete equality of human beginning in Genesis 1 with the account of Cain and Abel (Gen. 4:1–10) is illuminating. Cain and Abel, the sons of Adam and Eve, were a farmer and shepherd, respectively. Cain perceived that God preferred his sibling's offering over his own. This made Cain "very angry" (v. 5). He acted on his profound anger by murdering his own brother (v. 8). Importantly, this is the first mention of "sin" or wrongdoing in the Bible, which God indicated to

Cain was anthropomorphically "lurking at the door" while Cain was angry before his decision "not [to] do well" in killing Abel (v. 7).

The account of Cain and Abel is in part an etiological story of tribal hatred between shepherds and farmers running so deep that it affected brothers who shared blood in the ultimate way, by the shedding of blood. The summit of this ancient story is Cain's post-murder inquisitive answer to God asking the whereabouts of Abel: "Am I my brother's keeper?" (Gen. 4:9). The implicit answer in this formative anecdote is a resounding, divine "YES"— from the beginning and for all generations.

For me, the garden of Eden account (Gen. 2–3) of creation is more mysterious and ambiguous than combining Genesis 1 and 4 into a practical, understandable, and life-experience-authenticated beginning of equality and goodness; one actualized in good choices and spoiled by bad decisions. Yet, the Eden story is complementary by teaching us that we are mortal and that our lives will not be easy. Thus, time is of the essence in order to live each day with good choices rooted in loving and caring for our sisters and brothers, regardless of differences. This is what God ordained as "very good" from the beginning. God knows these choices are critically important for healing and progressing toward goodness in our world today.

Without question, Jesus understood that our mortal lives should be characterized by good daily choices grounded in love, care, and the pursuit of justice. The earliest Gospel, Mark, quickly shows us what Jesus was all about in his life. Mark summarizes Jesus's teaching as the "kingdom of God is at hand"; thus, it is time to "repent" (Mark 1:15). Repent means to so radically change that it is like turning around and following a different path. Jesus went in the opposite direction of many prominent and powerful leaders of his own Jewish tradition by championing people who were habitually despised and oppressed. For example, shortly after summing up Jesus's teachings, Mark tells us that a leper begged Jesus to help him: "If you choose, you can make me clean" (v. 40). Many healthy people oppressed the ill, erroneously thinking illness meant God had rejected them. No one dared go near a leper, yet Jesus immediately seized the opportunity by "touching" and helping him (v. 41). Jesus showed us the power of a good choice.

The Gospel of Luke offers a strong example of Jesus's relentless pursuit of justice for the needy and ill-treated. As noted above in the prior chapter focused on social justice, Jesus, full of God's Spirit, announced in a Nazareth synagogue that God had "anointed [him] to bring good news to the poor . . . to proclaim release to the captives and recovery of sight to the blind [and] to let the oppressed go free" (Luke 4:18–19). Another example is from the start of the Sermon on the Mount in Matthew (Matt. 5–7). Jesus declared at the outset of this longest collection of his teachings that the "poor," "meek," hungry," "peacemakers," and "those who are persecuted" are in fact the "blessed" ones (Matt. 5:3, 5–6, 9–10).

Like Jesus's actions and the pure intention of every decent human being of any stripe, our choices should be "anointed" and consistent with how God made us from the start—with equality and having special concern for those who suffer or have suffered through oppression. The time for our return is beyond ripe. Let's not delay in actively making a lasting difference in how we choose to live.

CHAPTER 19

Hope Is Potential That Can Be Realized

ope is a beautiful thing. Yet, what is "hope" in relation to an aspiration, vocation, or dream way of life? For example, from a faith or meaningful quality of life perspective, what does it mean to hope for a life filled with loving, caring, and compassionate behavior? Is it a possibility—something that might happen depending on circumstances—or more certain and intentional?

In her powerful and inspiringly raw memoir, *Bravey* (The Dial Press 2021), former Olympian, world class athlete, filmmaker, and actress Alexi Pappas asks an important question: "Why not believe in potential?" She asks this in her chapter titled "Love" in relation to dreams and goals in life. Our truly authentic objectives require "intention" and are "forever work[s] in progress." Pappas counsels wisely that "fear of failure is the surest way to fail . . . [because] you become fueled by desperation rather than passion."

In the final chapter of her book titled "For Those Who Dream," Pappas makes an important distinction between commitment and interest: "Chasing a dream means giving a hundred percent of what you have every day." That is true commitment, not mere interest, which can evaporate when the path toward a goal becomes overly challenging.

This wise framework fits so well for how we live daily. For me as a Christian, it relates to the priority of following the teachings and model of Jesus. Practically, as I have emphasized many times, that means consistently living a life of compassion, inclusivity, love, care, and the pursuit of justice for the poor and for others who are oppressed or disadvantaged. Whether one is a Christian, a devotee of another faith tradition, or simply a person highly motivated to live a life that leaves a positive footprint, consistently living these qualities is a "dream" and a high calling.

We might all hope that we can consistently live in such a manner, but it does not just happen. We must make it happen, regardless of the difficulties, temporary setbacks, and failures we experience along the way. It is a matter of our choice and intention, and beyond and above that, our hard work and all-out effort.

Distinguishing *interest* from *absolute commitment* is so important. The two are related and essentially sequential. Interest is a predecessor to commitment and potentially can give birth to it, but that is up to each person. The transformation to pure and consistent commitment is far from automatic. Definitive choice and discipline create the bridge from interest to daily commitment.

An example from a perspective of faith is the difference between a creedal affirmation or confession of faith and actively practicing by living one's faith. For a Christian, this would be the initial or periodic expression of belief or affirmation in Jesus as one's Lord (intention) versus progressively engaging in a lifetime of hard work by endeavoring to walk the difficult and narrow path of following Jesus as a disciple (commitment).

A more particular example from day-to-day living involves the pursuit of justice and equal treatment for all, especially those who are disadvantaged or subject to oppression in any way. As noted emphatically before, seeking justice is at the core of Jesus's example and teachings related to loving others, as well as a priority of other legitimate faith traditions and of those who are generally seeking to be a good person. In our culture, where prejudice and other manifestations of injustice currently run rampant, we need more champions actively committed to justice.

Let's suppose that a person is with a particular group of friends while someone from outside the group is present. This person might look, talk, or act differently from the others. If someone in the group makes an inappropriate remark or tells an insensitive joke about that difference, what happens within the group? Another person in the group feels a twinge of discomfort but stops short of reacting because no one was physically hurt or even "pushed around." Later, however, one-on-one with the recipient of the insensitivity, this person expresses deep regret, sincere disagreement with what happened, and apologizes to the person who was hurt by the remark. Such a response shows a level of caring and good intention, but the failure to speak up and denounce the derogatory treatment on the spot, before the entire group, exemplifies a lack of commitment.

There is no magic potion that will alleviate the acrimony and prejudice we continue to witness in our fractured and factious country. Things are not resolved that way, even with the best of intentions. Instead, taking the high road of living ethically and morally, including seeking justice, takes commitment to strenuous daily effort and serious recommitment when we fall short.

CHAPTER 20

Mentoring as an Expression of Light and Love

Mentoring is a beautiful thing. As mentor or mentee, and best yet as both, mentoring enriches our life's quality and experiences. From a faith perspective, a mentor is akin to a bright light that helps inform and illuminate the paths of others who pay attention, ask questions, absorb wisdom, and learn. In the Judeo-Christian tradition, light is an important concept. For example, in Isaiah 49, the prophet told the Jewish people in Babylonian exile to return to their land and become God's gift as "a light to the nations," meaning all people (Isa. 49:6). Similarly, Jesus taught his followers that they are the "light of the world" and should let it "shine" so that others can see their "good works" (Matt. 5:14–16).

A mentor is almost always a role model for us, even when the person does not know they are mentoring us. As with role models, we often want to imitate our mentors and follow similar paths as they have. Better yet, mentors go beyond simply modeling behavior by advising, guiding, and consulting with us based on their experience and expertise. Life without trusted mentors would be so much harder. Similarly, life without being a mentor would be less fulfilling. Mentoring is a special and fiduciary way of loving another person, a profound type of love and care that runs from mentor to mentee and vice versa.

Should we seek out mentors? Yes, we should intentionally seek them out for input and positive influence in all seasons of life. We should also let them know that we look up to them and appreciate them for their contributions to our lives. The mentor–mentee relationship has lifelong impact, and, in some cases, the relationship can blossom into the most unique type of friendship. In fact, the mentoring might end up flowing both ways.

The mere concept of being a mentor and using the power of our imagination can enhance the quality of our daily lives. For all we know, some people around us each day might look to us as their models (without telling us) for learning and potentially patterning their behavior after ours. That can be both a frightening and exhilarating realization! Yet, if we wake up each day and simply imagine that some people we encounter routinely, such as at our workplace or school, look to us and closely observe us as mentors, it can have a profound and positive influence on our own behavior.

Living as if others are watching our behavior, words, and reactions can motivate us to pay heightened attention to how we live each moment and how we treat other people. It can help us model highly ethical and moral living, perhaps similar to what we observe in our own mentors and role models.

In his letter to the Ephesians, written before any of the New Testament Gospels, the apostle Paul may have borrowed from some of the oral traditions of Jesus's sayings as well as from his own Jewish tradition. Paul tells each of his readers that "you are light. Live as children of light—for the fruit of the light is found in all that is good and right and true" (Eph. 5:8–9). Earlier in Ephesians, Paul says God made us "for good works . . . to be our way of life" (Eph. 2:10). Good works and being a light to others are intertwined.

We are all God's children and can choose to be a light to others by intentionally living daily in love, showing care for other people through active, consistent good works. We can also make good choices of those we select to help us along our path of life so that our own behavior improves. It can be motivational to think of others watching us and being impacted by how we live, regardless of whether anyone is actually looking. Whether other people are paying attention to us or not (and we would be surprised to learn how often they do), the belief that others are attentive to our every move can be quite motivational. It can help us think before we speak, pause before we react, and otherwise truly live with good intention.

We do not have forever to be a mentor, to seek out mentors to help us, or to do our best to set a good example for those around us. Returning to Ephesians, we see Paul follow up his reminder that we are a light to others with some profound wisdom about actualizing good intention during our limited time with a passage I repeatedly emphasize: "Be careful then how you live, not as unwise people but as wise, making the most of the time" (Eph. 5:15–16).

How much time do we have? We have today and now, so let's not hesitate to shine a bright light for others and to always seek out the brightest lights as models for our own lives.

Mindfulness: Religious Roots and Select Clinical Observations

RELIGIOUS ROOTS OF MINDFULNESS

The origin and development of the practice of mindfulness is a substantial subject well beyond the scope of this appendix. Nevertheless, I offer some comments and observations, emphasizing that striving toward full attention is an ongoing process. This brief input relates primarily to the Buddhist beginnings of mindfulness and its expansion beyond Buddhism to the West, as well as a few comments on clinically based utilization of mindfulness to assist and promote individual practices. This limited information about the origin and practice of mindfulness highlights its vital importance to the ethical practice of life.

The beginnings of mindfulness start with Buddhism and Buddha himself. Buddha was born in the middle of the sixth century BCE.[2] In Huston Smith's foundational work, *The Religions*

---

2. Huston Smith, *The Religions of Man* (New York: Harper & Row First Perennial Library Ed., 1965), 91.

of Man, first published in 1958, he emphasizes Buddha's[3] answer when asked who he was: "I am awake."[4] Per Smith, that is what "Buddha" means. The Sanskrit root includes both waking up and knowing.[5] In a nutshell, being fully awake, with knowledge and complete awareness in the present, is the heart of being mindful or what we can simply call "focused."

According to Smith, Buddha taught "a religion of intense self-effort."[6] He encouraged "the way of intentional living [that] he called the Path,"[7] which included "right mindfulness" as one key to such a path.[8] Living with such an intentional daily and momentary focus in *any* time or place requires hard personal work and consistency. A refined and intentional practice helps us make singular focus into more of a habit over time. Such discipline and commitment are noble pursuits toward a narrow path of life indeed. Like other religions, including Judaism and Christianity,[9] Buddhism is multi-faceted. It is divided into certain threads or schools.[10] One of these schools that continues to exert profound influence on Western thought is Zen Buddhism.[11] *Zen* means "the meditation that leads to insight."[12]

Although Buddhism is technically an Eastern religion, Zen ideas have significantly and positively informed the West. Below

---

3. The Buddha's full name was Siddhartha Gautama of the Sakyas. He was born in northern India about 560 BCE.

4. Ibid., 90.

5. Ibid.

6. Ibid., 107.

7. Ibid., 116.

8. Ibid., 121.

9. Christianity is split into Eastern and Western; Western split into Catholic and Protestant—there have been multiple splits otherwise and within each of these.

10. Ibid., 132. (and note 9 and 11).

11. Buddhism split into two significant branches, Mahayana and Theravada, shortly after the death of Buddha. Zen is one of several schools or ways deriving from the Mahayana line.

12. Ibid., 139–40. (and note 11)

are a few examples with perspectives on mindfulness in religious and clinical settings.

Thich Nhat Hanh is a popular Zen author and advocate who has garnered significant influence around the world, including in the West. Taking what he learned as a Vietnamese peace advocate in the 1960s, Hanh became a prolific author of Zen-related books.[13] In recognition of his incredible work for peace, Martin Luther King, Jr. nominated Hanh for the Nobel Peace Prize in 1967.[14] Thomas Merton, a well-known American Catholic leader, prolific writer (with substantial impact within and outside of Christianity), 1960s-era social justice activist, and monk, called Hanh "his brother."[15] Merton was open and ecumenical in his approach to Christianity and other faith traditions. He embraced Zen and other Eastern religious ideas, emphasizing common ground and parallels to Christianity.[16] Hanh also embraced commonalities with Christianity.[17]

In one of Hanh's excellent books, *The Miracle of Mindfulness: An Introduction to the Practice of Meditation*,[18] Hanh notes that he "use[s] the term 'mindfulness' to refer to keeping one's consciousness alive to the present reality."[19] Further, "[m]indfulness frees us of forgetfulness and dispersion," which offers the potential to truly live in the moment.[20]

---

13. Thich Nhat Hanh, *Peace is Every Step*, ed. Arnold Kotler (New York: Bantam Books, 1992), x-xv.

14. Ibid., xi.

15. Thich Nhat Hanh, *Living Buddha, Living Christ*, 10th Anniversary ed., David Steindl-Rast, Foreword
(New York: Penguin Group, 2007), xiii–xiv.

16. Amiya Chakravarty, consulting ed., *The Asian Journal of Thomas Merton* (New York: New Directions Publishing, 1973), *supra* note28, 311.

17. Thich Nhat Hanh, *Living Buddha, Living Christ* ed., David Steindl-Rast, note 14, at xvii.

18. Thich Nhat Hanh, *The Miracle of Mindfulness: An Introduction to the Practice of Meditation*, Mobi Ho, trans., (Boston, MA: Beacon Press 1975), 7.

19. Ibid., 11.

20. Ibid., 15.

OBSERVATIONS ON CLINICAL UTILIZATION OF MINDFULNESS

What we might describe as the clinical and health-related practice of mindfulness easily blends into its religious foundations.

Lorne Ladner is a clinical psychologist and professor. He directs a Buddhist center in Virginia, encouraging and utilizing a dialogue of sorts between Buddhism and Western psychology in his book, *The Lost Art of Compassion*.[21] According to Ladner at the start of this work:

> Buddhist masters always have emphasized that each moment of life is precious. In any given moment, we can allow life to pass us by or we can be mindful of what's most essential, living with genuine purpose, energy, and joy. . . . When we're aware and awake in a given moment, we have the capacity to make that moment extraordinary.[22]

Ladner also highlights Tibetan traditions for "cultivating compassion," and "the ideas and methods so freely offered by the Mahayana Buddhist traditions of Central Asia.

In *Full Catastrophe Living*, Jon Kabat-Zinn includes a wealth of detailed information about the positive, health-based benefits of mindfulness.[23] In his "Introduction to the Second Edition," Dr. Kabat-Zinn explains that his comprehensive work primarily keys off of the Mindfulness-Based Stress Reduction program associated with the Stress Reduction Clinic at the University of Massachusetts Medical Center.[24] Notably, and representative of the inherent link between the importance of practicing

---

21. Lorne Ladner, *The Lost Art of Compassion* (San Francisco: Harper 2004), xiii, xvii.

22. Ibid., 3.

23. Jon Kabat-Zinn, *Full Catastrophe Living* (New York: Bantam Books, 2013), 169.

24. Ibid., xxv–xlvii.

mindfulness in religious and clinical contexts, Thich Nhat Hanh offers endorsing comments in the preface to the first and second editions of Dr. Kabat-Zinn's work: "This [is a] very readable and practical book [that] will be helpful in many ways. . . . This book's invitation for each one of us to wake up and savor every moment we are given to live has never been more needed than it is today."[25]

Dr. Kabat-Zinn describes mindfulness as "not merely a concept [but] a *way of being*" that is "akin to wisdom."[26] Further, regarding our perspectives on stress, he says, "[W]e don't have to make the sources of our stress go away. . . . [Rather,] we can change our attitude and thereby our relationship to our circumstances."[27]

In *Trauma Stewardship*, social worker and workshop educator Laura van Dernoot Lipsky addresses the effects of trauma exposure and the compelling need to deal with it in part through self-care.[28] In her chapter titled "Choosing Our Focus," she quotes Marcel Proust, a French novelist: "The real voyage of discovery consists not in seeking new landscapes but in having *new eyes*."[29] That powerful statement emphasizes the importance of personal choice. We decide and control our attention and attitudes in life, including within our work lives. According to Ms. Lipsky, "There is great power in understanding that we can change the way we interact with circumstances in our lives, simply by being intentional about where we put our focus."[30] She further observes that "there is a real likelihood that with time and practice, a temporary,

---

25. Ibid., xxiiv

26. Ibid., xxxv (emphasis added).

27. Ibid, xxxvi.

28. Laura van Dernoot Lipsky, *Trauma Stewardship: An Everyday Guide to Caring for Self While Caring for Others* (Oakland, CA: Berrett-Koehler Publishers, 2009), 132–33.

29. Ibid., 172 (emphasis added).

30. Ibid., 175.

intentionally created mindful state will become a lasting mental trait."[31]

Our attitude toward circumstances is of ultimate importance to our mindset and focus on daily working and living. In his autobiographical work, *Man's Search for Meaning*, Viktor Frankl describes his experiences and survival in the horrific context of the concentration camp at Auschwitz during World War II. This important and well-known first English translation was originally published in 1959 under the more compelling title *From Death Camp to Existentialism*.[32]

Dr. Frankl certainly deserves our attention in suggesting how to cope with stressful and difficult circumstances. According to his experiential reflections during his time in Auschwitz, he advises, "[E]verything can be taken from a [person] but one thing; the last of human freedoms—*to choose one's attitude in any given set of circumstances,* to choose one's own way."[33]

Dr. Frankl was a renowned psychiatrist and is known in part as the founder of the "third Viennese school of psychotherapy" (after Freud and Adler).[34] Dr. Frankl's "school" is often referred to as Logotherapy, which generally keys into meaning in life.[35] It is a "meaning-centered Psychotherapy."[36] The 2006 republication of *Man's Search for Meaning* includes a helpful extended section titled "Logotherapy in a Nutshell."[37]

31. Ibid.

32. Victor E. Frankl, *Man's Search for Meaning*, Ilse Lasch trans. (Boston, MA: Beacon Press 2006), iv.

33. Ibid., 66 (emphasis added).

34. Marius Schneider, "The Existentialistic Concept of the Human Person in Viktor E. Frankl's Logotherapy," *Heirs and Ancestors*, John Ryan, ed. (Washington, DC: Catholic University of America Press 2018), 39–64.

35. Frankl, *supra* note 32, 98.

36. Ibid.

37. Ibid., 97–134.

APPENDIX 2

Practical Considerations: Developing New Habits

Affirming the excellence of mindfulness as a concept is one thing. Translating it into something practical and beneficial, including in our respective workplaces and all other contexts, is quite another.

Moving toward a focused, present-oriented personal and work life will always be a work in progress. It takes discipline, hard work, and time. Developing an efficient and consistent daily routine that becomes a habit over time is most helpful, as are daily reminders to refocus our attention as we inevitably slip into an all-encompassing mode of multi-tasking.

In his helpful book *The Inner Athlete*, Dan Millman addresses the time commitment of changing an existing practice or adopting a new routine:

> In changing to a new pattern of . . . life habits, the initiatory period may last from one to six weeks or even longer. By the end of that time, we'll have adapted to a new pattern. The period of stabilization, however, takes from three to six months. During this period, it's important to maintain

our desire, motivation, and commitment by visualizing the goal—by letting it inspire us.[38]

I recall when I started running over forty years ago, starting at the YMCA then heading through a local park, a wise older runner counseled me that if I was truly serious about running as a daily habit, I needed to commit to the process for six months before deciding whether to stick to it. I wanted to quit in the early months, but by three or four months I was hooked on how much I loved it and how much it contributed to my life quality, serenity, productivity, and efficiency. Later, it became a meditative vehicle as well, as I discuss below in my comments about working on helpful practices in life, including trying to create and refine them. Developing exercise habits is hard enough; working toward focused and balanced practices to improve all aspects of our lives is especially challenging. We should consider such hard work a lifelong process.

In *Trauma Stewardship*, Ms. Lipsky importantly observes that "a practice is not just a healthy option; it is our best hope of creating a truly sustainable life for ourselves."[39] She stresses that the "more we remind ourselves of this, the more likely we are to discover the discipline we need."[40] Ms. Lipsky simplifies this by suggesting two steps: "The first is to create an intention for your day, and the second is to begin to *cultivate moments of mindfulness.*"[41]

From a personal practice perspective, I have experimented with several daily practices and reminder routines throughout each day in order to stay alert, focused, and relaxed. I make progress, then fall and get back up to refine and work harder. Currently, I get up very early and start my day with activities designed to focus my attention fully on the moment. My intention and hope are that the early morning routine influences my entire day. At some point in my life, it occurred to me that if I did not *start* my day in such a manner, then I would have little if any chance to make effective changes each day.

My current routine consists of about thirty to forty-five minutes of solace, with coffee beside me and my dog in my lap. When I was younger, I spent less time, maybe fifteen to twenty minutes. During this time, I slowly

---

38. Dan Millman, *The Inner Athlete: Realizing Your Full Potential* (Walhole, NH: Stillpoint Publishing 1994), 82.

39. Lipsky, *supra* note 28, 230.

40. Ibid.

41. Ibid., 231 (emphasis added).

read short excerpts of meaningful life-oriented books or articles, followed with prayerful meditation or simply being quiet and still. I do all of this very early in the morning when I first get up, either in my study (using the same chair I have for years) or on our screened-in porch. I then follow it with a habit I developed even earlier: running and/or walking. Mentally, I look at this as an extension of my time for mental stillness and preparation for the day. I work through some familiar and meaningful words each day as I run. If I have trouble during the day, I endeavor to recall these words and the quiet and solitude I experienced earlier that same day as a way of calling to mind the perspective I set for myself. For me, starting with a daily practice and then recalling parts of it during the day are essential for habitual intention, focus, and balance. When the specific activities in my routine grow ineffective or stale, then I experiment with changes for greater effectiveness.

As a personal note, I benefit substantially from preparing and implementing short, doable lists of points or steps for intentionally approaching the day, a segment of it, or a particular task within it. My lists are the old-school kind: I prepare them with a pen on paper as opposed to utilizing "smart" communication/ electronic devices. This approach helps me *slow down*, which itself is a good starting point for any day. I use short lists, a technique I learned from decades as a law professor and practitioner. For example, I make a short list of steps to follow in each class I teach. I am better at making the lists, however, than I am at mindfully walking through them one item at a time.

An agenda is helpful if we truly see only one thing—better yet, one moment—at a time. Problems arise, however, when we think too much about all the planned activities ahead of us, when we question and rethink the steps we have already taken, or when we speculate on what is yet to come. A daily plan with a reasonable number of objectives to accomplish can facilitate being mindful, but completion of the list should not be a dominant concern. We should be flexible and willing to react to unexpected developments in line with our priorities during any day.

Over the years, to drill better habits into my mind and actions, I began adding words and phrases (written in all capitals) to the top of my daily lists, such as *slow, clarity,* and *be where you are and make it count.* After all, we should realize that *how* we do each thing (quality) is more significant than *how much* we do (quantity).

Hanh and Ladner offer practical and applicable wisdom in the works noted above in Appendix 1. Regarding the importance of doing one thing at a time, Hanh suggests:

> Whatever the tasks, do them slowly and with ease, in mindfulness. Don't do any task in order to get it over with. Resolve to do each job in a relaxed way, with all your attention. . . . No matter [the] task . . . do it slowly and evenly, without reluctance.[42]

Enhancing these thoughts about deliberate focus and action, Ladner observes:

> We spend so much of our time doing things automatically that it is important to assess . . . our habits. . . . Whenever we think that how we spend a given . . . hour is unimportant, and whenever we think we need to rush through what we're doing so that later we can get to something more relaxing, meaningful, or important, we are cheating ourselves.[43]

---

42. Hanh, *supra* note 18, 29.
43. Ladner, *supra* note 21, 4.

In addition to cheating ourselves, we are also potentially neglecting other people who may be affected and influenced by our activities.

Ms. Lipsky encourages us to "[n]ever underestimate what [we] can weave into [our] . . . work or career [or life] to make it a healthier place for [us] to be. Decide that being a martyr in [any context] is a thing of the past."[44] She further emphasizes that "we are only *a benefit to those we serve* if we are able to have some true balance in our life."[45] Thus, consistently working toward habits that help us stay focused within a life of balanced priorities is critical to ethically serving others' best interests, along with our own.

In our modern world, filled with endless demands and smart, quick communicative devices, communication presents special challenges. Although it is not easy, Ladner reminds us that "any of us can pause in this moment to consider what's most essential and then live this moment in a *deliberate* [and] *meaningful* . . . way."[46]

Pausing before we communicate is such a helpful concept, practice, and habit, especially when responding to criticism and negative comments that either are or feel like personal affronts. This applies regardless of the mode of communication, although it can be more difficult with texting (or any other means of frequent, persistent, and immediate response). Contemporarily, there is a permanent imprint of everything we say regardless of how we communicate it. This enhances our need for utilizing great care before communicating with anyone, especially in a reactive mode.

Developing a habitual, intentional, and consistent practice benefits the tone and quality of our communication skills. It allows us to be mindful both when we communicate and when we

---

44. Lipsky, *supra* note 28, 211.
45. Ibid. (emphasis added).
46. Ladner, *supra* note 21, 4 (emphasis added).

decide it is best to keep quiet. As a suggested responsive framework, especially to negative comments seemingly directed toward us, consider a routine that includes:

1. Pausing (instead of a gut-reaction emotional response);
2. Reflecting and processing;
3. Simply breathing easily to calm ourselves;
4. Reflecting again, including considering potential consequences of our response choices.

After going through this or a similar routine, we can often better decide whether to respond at all, and if so, how and with what tone and attitude.

Focus and balance deteriorate without consistent reminders to slow down a bit in life. Not slowing down allows chaos to set in. This is especially true in difficult seasons of our lives. Mindfulness is a foundation of a truly authentic, meaningful, and happy life.

Bibliography

Abrams, Douglas, *The Book of Joy* (Avery/Penguin Random House, New York, 2016).

Frankl, Viktor, *Man's Search for Meaning*, Ilse Lasch trans. (Beacon Press, Boston, MA, 2006). (Originally published in 1959 Original title: *From Death Camp to Existentialism*.)

Hanh, Thich Nhat, *Living Buddha, Living Christ* (Riverhead Books, 1995).

Hanh, Thich Nhat, *The Miracle of Mindfulness: An Introduction to the Practice of Meditation*, Mobi Ho, trans. (Beacon Press, 1975).

Hanh, Thich Nhat, *Peace is Every Step*, ed. Arnold Kotler (Bantam Books, 1992).

Kabat-Zinn, Dr. Jon, *Full Catastrophe Living* (Bantam Books, 2013).

Kushner, Rabbi Harold, *Conquering Fear: Living Boldly in an Uncertain World* (Anchor Books, Cottonwood, AZ, 2010).

Kushner, Rabbi Harold, *When All You've Ever Wanted Isn't Enough* (Pocket Books, 1986).

Kushner, Rabbi Harold, *When Bad Things Happen to Good People* (Avon Books, 1981).

Ladner, Lorne, *The Lost Art of Compassion* (Harper San Francisco, 2004).

Lipsky, Laura van Dernoot, *Trauma Stewardship: An Everyday Guide to Caring for Self While Caring for Others* (Berrett-Koehler Publishers, Inc. 2009).

Millman, Dan, *The Inner Athlete: Realizing Your Full Potential* (Stillpoint Publishing, New Hampshire, 1994).

Pappas, Alexi, *Bravey* (Dial Press, 2021).

Penick, Harvey, *And If You Play Golf, You're My Friend* (Simon & Schuster, 1993).

Penick, Harvey, *Harvey Penick's Little Red Book* (Simon & Schuster, New York, 1992).

Schneider, Marius, *Heirs and Ancestors,* "The Existentialistic Concept of the Human Person" in Viktor E. Frankl's *Logotherapy* (Catholic University of America Press, 2018).

Smith, Huston, *The Religions of Man* (Harper & Row, First Perennial Library Ed. 1965).

Acknowledgements

I have so many people to thank, so this list is incomplete. With that in mind, I express heartfelt gratitude to:

The many readers of my first book, *The Daily Practice of Life: Practical Reflections Toward Meaningful Living* (CrossLink Publishing 2020), as well as readers of my *Austin American-Statesman* faith and life quality columns, who encouraged me to write another book.

The professionals at CrossLink Publishing, including Rick Bates and Matthew Doan, for their support, encouragement, and expertise in improving the quality of my book and for providing an awesome, "author friendly" process and atmosphere.

Mindy Reed for her expertise, developmental edit of my initial draft manuscript, friendship, and encouragement to keep writing.

Nicole Villalpando of the *Austin American-Statesman*, for her long-time support and encouragement of all my writing ventures, including and especially my *Statesman* columns.

Howard Miller, my favorite teacher, mentor, and now great friend, for honoring me by writing the foreword to my book.

All my friends at The Church at Highland Park in Austin, Texas, including our pastors, Cheryl Kimble and Masyn Evans-Clements, and all members of our Sunday morning discussion group, for their unwavering support, encouragement, and count-less positive influences on my personal faith journey.

All my expert friends at Zilker Media in Austin (including my son, Rusty, and Shelby Janner in particular) for their promotion-al efforts related to all my writing and speaking ventures.

My brother, Rusty, for being the best of brothers and friends and for his constant support, encouragement, and gentle sugges-tions and ideas as an English professor related to my writing.

My children, Courtney Morton and Rusty Shelton, for their love and strong support and help related to my writing and every aspect of my life.

Last on this incomplete list but #1 on all my lists and more so in my heart, my wife and forever companion, Roxanne.

About the Author

Walt Shelton is a prolific writer, speaker, and group leader on faith and life-quality related matters. This is his second book. He is also the author of the Nautilus Award-winning book, *The Daily Practice of Life: Practical Reflections Toward Meaningful Living* (CrossLink Publishing 2020). Walt is one of the most read faith columnists in Texas over the last decade, with more than sixty columns published in the *Austin American-Statesman*.

Walt is passionate about practical applications of faith, inclusivity, compassion, and actively pursuing justice. He is a committed Christian and understands Christianity as being all about following the life-model and teachings of Jesus as discerned in prominent, consistent themes of the New Testament, especially the Gospels, as well as the best of Jesus's tradition and what Jesus utilized and exhibited as a Jewish rabbi. Walt is a strong advocate of learning from and finding common ground with other faith traditions.

As a professor at Baylor Law School for more than thirty years, Walt is passionate for both his vocation and his never-ending interest in encouraging and empowering current and former students through knowledge, communication, introspection, and friendship. Walt is blessed that the encouragement and friendship run both ways, as he continues to learn and grow from what students teach and show him.

In legal circles, although he currently practices very little, Walt is a nationally recognized environmental and water law attorney and speaker. His legal realm foci in recent years have been speaking and writing about ethical issues related to applicable standards for attorneys and more so the importance of balancing personal priorities and quality of life considerations in such a demanding and often time-consuming profession. Walt also devotes substantial time to service in the legal community, especially as it relates to law students across Texas. As the long-time chair and now co-chair of the Environmental and Natural Resources Law Section of the State Bar of Texas, among other activities, Walt organizes and participates in law school programs and other educational initiatives at all law schools in Texas.

Walt has been happily married to Roxanne Shelton for forty-three years and counting. They have two children, five grandchildren, and one very special rescue dachshund (Walt's breed of choice for life), all in the Austin area.

For more information, please visit www.WaltShelton.com.